T0114423

Praise for

FAR APPALACHIA

"[*Far Appalachia*] is utterly unpretentious—simple, memorable, and beautiful." —*Booklist*

"Full of . . . quiet, and often unexpected grace . . . in easygoing and understated prose, [Adams] takes readers up the river with him . . . he skims lightly over the depths and navigates the rapids with humor and a sharp eye for detail." —*Publishers Weekly*

"A lyrical journey through the heart of the mountain South." —Sharyn McCrumb, author of *The Songcatcher*

"A compelling personal narrative of documentary observation that becomes, finally, a talented writer's generous gift to his readers." —Robert Coles, author of *Children in Crisis*

"The New [River], while steeped in heritage, isn't a deep river in most places. Its tranquil appearance belies its power, and it carries you swiftly along. So does Adams' book." —*The Roanoke Times*

"[*Far Appalachia*] is deceptive; as easily read as water slipping between your fingers, its undercurrents holding much longer." —*The Courier Journal* (Louisville, Ky.)

"Listeners of National Public Radio are familiar with Noah Adams's rich, evenly paced voice. . . . Now readers have an opportunity to discover [his] other voice—equally self-assured, moderate, and mellifluous . . ." —*BookPage*

Praise for Noah Adams's
PIANO LESSONS

"Charming . . . his delight in music-making is palpable."
—*The New Yorker*

"[A] charming memoir . . . Adams clearly possesses a gift that too
many teachers don't—the ability to convey just how much fun
it is to make music, and just how many different ways there are
for a piece of music to be beautiful." —*Newsday*

"An affectionate tribute . . . [from] a writer of
considerable merit." —*The Seattle Times*

"Entertaining and surprising detail . . . *Piano Lessons* will make
you a believer in the quest to find and make music and will
have you falling back in love with your own dreams, whatever
they may be." —John Hockenberry, correspondent,
ABC News, author of *Moving Violations*

"A truly absorbing story . . . [told] with humor and candor . . .
Adams is a gifted interviewer with a good ear for a story, and
Piano Lessons is full of them." —*Minneapolis Star Tribune*

"Genuinely moving . . . Adams writes in the same earnest . . .
tone that has endeared him to radio listeners for more than
twenty years." —*San Francisco Examiner & Chronicle*

"The balance of storytelling—about pianos specifically,
and then into music in general and back again—rings
nicely, with plenty of pushed pedals to sustain it."
—*The Philadelphia Inquirer*

NOAH ADAMS

FAR
APPALACHIA

FOLLOWING THE
NEW RIVER NORTH

DELTA TRADE PAPERBACKS

A Delta Book
Published by
Dell Publishing
a division of
Random House, Inc.
New York, New York

ISBN: 978-0-385-32013-9

Library of Congress Catalog Card Number: 00-048506

Reprinted by arrangement with Delacorte Press

Published simultaneously in Canada

CONTENTS

CONTENTS

PREFACE

I had the good fortune of being able to leave work for close to a year, to follow the New River on its course out of North Carolina. It's a river I'd wondered about—you cross it fast on I-77 and I-81 in Virginia, and I-64 in West Virginia, with no chance even to see the water. One day, looking at the atlas, I noticed the thin, blue traces of the New, and realized the river could be the slower way into the country that I'd been looking for.

I was born in Ashland, Kentucky, a medium-sized steel mill town in the northeastern corner of the state, at the edge of Appalachia. Our house was five blocks away from the Ohio River, which then ran muddy and oily, hidden away behind a floodwall, with tugboats pushing coal barges out of West Virginia. We had chemical and coke plants nearby too, and the sky over the broad valley at night could be lit sulfurous by the ovens and the natural gas flames.

I knew little of my family's background. One grandfather became a storekeeper, after farming. The other worked for the steel company but dreamed of railroading. My grandmothers were a generation or so away from cabin homesteads in West Virginia and Kentucky. The lumber, the railroads, the oil and coal, drew them all together in the towns.

I left home in 1962, starting my career in radio. After I came to NPR in Washington in 1975, I would often return on reporting trips, starting to learn more about the region. I went into the coalfields of eastern Kentucky and West Virginia for stories about strikes, and the effects of strip mining, and for interviews with writers and musicians. The assignments could be frustrating—you'd only have a couple of days, traveling and talking to people.

The New River wanders east and west but mostly flows north through Appalachia, and that can be confusing since it's hard to think of "south" as being "upriver." The name, it's thought, comes from pioneer surveyors, making note of a "new river." It is about 350 river miles from the mountaintop where the North Fork begins to the point in West Virginia where the New ends. I traveled most of that distance, and much of the South Fork as well, on the water or on trails. Some parts of the New I've been down many times, some not at all. And I've spent long days driving slowly, meeting people and talking with them—it's hard to find out much about a river if you stay in the center of the current. In the pages to follow you'll find the experiences of many trips set in the narrative form of a single river ad-

venture, moving from the headwaters to the final confluence, and from late spring to early fall.

This is just a book about a river. There was no quest involved, only a wish to understand more about this part of
the country and my family's past. It was a year of wonderful travels, and, in case you have a chance to follow some
of the route yourself, I've included the latitude and longi-
tude for each chapter's location. If you go, I promise you'll
find a much deeper story. I think of my book as just "the
angels' share." That's what the whisky makers of Scotland
and then Appalachia call the tiny amount of the essence
that escapes from the still as vapor into the mountain air.

1
___

SNAKE MOUNTAIN

36° 20'N
81° 42'W

I had a dream one night, not long ago, that I saw Doc Watson canoeing over a mountain in the dark. He was in the middle of the boat and doing some strong paddling. His head was tilted down a little bit, to the right. You couldn't tell he was blind; his eyes were intent. There was moonlight in his hair.

Mr. Watson was coming off the crest of a ridge riding a fast, splashing current. I still haven't questioned how the canoe got over the mountain or how the river contrived to be running uphill. The joy of the dream was that he was out for a ride—sensing the full moon, leaning into each stroke with the water cold on his arms.

He would be listening to the river's gurgle and plonk and the bell-toned night call of the Carolina wren. He'd recognize the black oak's leaf rustle. And there'd come the faint cry of a baby, from back up in the trees: most likely the wind but some might say a cougar.

The sounds would gather into guitar chords and

melody, and later Doc would play someplace in town, play a song like "Deep River Blues," and somebody standing against the back wall would shake his head and say, "It's like he just finds the music in the air."

I recognized the terrain of this dream: Snake Mountain reaches above five thousand feet in a corner of North Carolina and it would stand clear in a moonlit sky. Doc Watson lives in Deep Gap, not far away.

He grew up not being able to see but he heard the very center of music in the bird songs and the wind harmonies in the white pines along the pastures. Once he strung a wire in the barn so that it would sound a C and he could find songs on it. The Grand Ole Opry would be on the radio Saturday nights and later he heard enough rock and roll to be thought of as an electric guitar player but the old-time music held strong.

When all the family would come together after church they'd play the remembered tunes; an uncle would get his fiddle from the truck, one of the girls would lay out a dulcimer. The talk would be of mountains and farming. It was two close centuries ago that a Watson forebear left the Scottish Highlands.

Doc's grandmother, summer afternoons on the front porch, liked to sing hymns as she snapped the green beans for supper:

O, they tell me of a home far beyond the skies,
O, they tell me of a home far away;

O, they tell me of a home where no storm clouds rise,
O, they tell me of an unclouded day.

The North Carolina map in the glove box of my Jeep is a depiction of roads, a drawing of landscapes dominated by highways. Back at the turn of the century a map would feature the rail lines. And earlier still, in Daniel Boone's time, the maps were of *waterways*—territories defined by the creeks and rivers curving through the hills.

If you squint a bit you can find the New River on the modern state maps, and follow it north. It rises both in Watauga and Ashe Counties, in northwestern North Carolina, then becomes a single line winding into Virginia past Galax, through Radford, and over to the town of Narrows before entering West Virginia and moving up to Hinton, Prince, and Fayetteville, then ending at Gauley Bridge, where the New and Gauley Rivers join as the Kanawha. From there, downstream, run the broad meanderings of the Ohio, the Mississippi.

Move up to a larger-scale map—the U.S. Geological Survey 1:24 000 topographic—and you'll find the actual beginnings of the New (even the houses are shown, as tiny black squares).

The river's origin is divided. Look at the Boone Quadrangle map to find where the South Fork gets its start, up near the town of Blowing Rock. The water comes off the hillside and down through a golf course. It's just below the Blue Ridge Parkway, along the Eastern Continental

Divide; rain falling on the other side of the road would head toward the Atlantic.

The golf course outside of Blowing Rock marks the southernmost flow of the New, the farthest from the river's end, and some would call that the source point. Other geographers—the ones I agree with—say the *highest* source is where you mark the beginning of a river. And that takes us to the Zionville Quadrangle, to locate the North Fork, on Snake Mountain.

One morning in sunshine I drove up a narrow, newly paved road, then a twistier stone-and-dirt path, for a visit with a couple—Dave and Betty Martin—who spend every summer just below Snake Mountain's rounded peak. They have a weathered wooden shed, a dependable garden, nearby spring water, and, at the moment, two dogs.

"Hey there, morning." Dave and Betty had the same crinkly, tanned smile, and gray hair touched with white. It was past nine o'clock and they'd slept late. They wore jeans. They were barefoot. The dogs snuffled and pranced in the drying grass.

The summit of Snake Mountain is at 5,574 feet. Tennessee is on the other side. There are beech trees along the top ridge and sugar and red maples below. The hillside is in pasture, the scattered hay bales—the summer's first cutting—stand drying. Dave Martin sees this with a painter's eye, in pale blues, veiled white, muted greens and browns.

He brought out some of his watercolor work, done on scroll paper with Chinese brushes. The lines circled and soared—clouds became falling water and trees became forest.

Much later, when I was back at home looking at a series of topo maps on the wall, I was reminded of Dave's paintings; the *rhythm* was the same, the wanderings of the hills and watercourses. The only harsh, nonlyrical lines on the maps were those showing the highways and power lines.

Dave said he'd had a show of his watercolors once, "off the mountain"—an exhibit in the North Carolina city where they live. He was disappointed in the paintings. Vibrancy was lost. The light was off somehow. The next summer he brought them back to Snake Mountain, where they revived.

This year the Martins have been grumbling about the state's decision to pave the back-county road that climbs past the turnoff to their cabin. "What the highway department never tells you is that the gravel roads don't kill people, can't get up enough speed. If a drunk goes off the road he just goes into a fence."

Back down the mountain two miles is a community settled long ago by families that tended to differ.

"Pottertown," Dave says, "has the worst reputation in the hills of people feuding, or shooting their relatives. Up until about ten years ago the police wouldn't come over here except on Sunday afternoons. For us, one of the most interesting things in coming back every spring was finding out who'd been killed. They're still clannish; they tell these stories that happened a hundred years ago and get the young people all fired up. We've made good friends though, and we've always felt safe. Never lost anything, never had anything stolen. Most of the people who would tend to rob you would be afraid to come over here."

The Martins bought their land on Snake Mountain almost thirty years ago and they come up from the city in June. The garden's the first chore. They wouldn't want to bother with a real house, or plumbing. The only light they see at night is flickering thirty miles away on Mount Rogers. Dave figures this is the healthiest place they can be; they never get sick up here.

There are several springs above 4,700 feet, Dave said, that help start the New River's North Fork. " 'Bold springs,' the local people call them." We walked across a field to the "household" spring. The spot was sheltered by several Fraser firs. Dave and Betty had collected rocks to build a catch basin and encouraged spearmint and peppermint and mountain mint. I dipped out some water with a plastic cup and drank most of it, splashing the rest on my face. It held the chill of the rock. The water from this spring would find its way down to the creek, to the rivers, to the Gulf of Mexico, and rise again in the clouds to fall on Snake Mountain.

2

THREE FORKS

36° 13′N
81° 38′W

The sycamore tree became my first friend on the river, in the sense that I'd know its name without looking. The gray-green scaly sycamores stand as sentinels along the entire course of the New; often they'll lean far out over the water.

And jewelweed was the first wildflower I identified from a field guidebook. Until October, where there's water flowing, you can usually find jewelweed. They are plants for a hobbit's landscape, with reddish orange blossoms that look like tiny pitchers. You can crush the stems and use the juice against poison ivy. In the fall the seedpods will burst open at a touch and send out a satisfying spray.

It's good to find a color picture in a book that matches what's blooming on the riverbank. But often I wanted to *stop* the water's flow and wait right in the middle of the stream. I could tell I was paddling past tiny, unseen worlds.

A biologist agreed to help. For Ed Greene it was a chance to leave his office at Appalachian State University and get his feet in the river. We picked a shallow section close to the town of Boone and the ASU campus, just downstream from where the South Fork becomes complete, with the joining of the Middle Fork, East Fork, and Winkler Creek.

We walked a half-mile trail from the parking area to the water, and Ed made sure I noticed the neighborhood trees:

"Wild cherry. There's witch hazel; it can be a bush but it gets to a pretty good size. And you know your white pine. There's another cherry—see the bagworms? They'll hit a cherry more than anything else. Here's a sweet birch. It's a toothbrush tree; just fray this twig there at the end and it works great. Hawthorns there, with the big sharp thorns. Red oak. Lots of black locust; people call it a trash tree and mostly it is, but if you want fence posts that won't rot that's the wood for you."

Ed enjoyed seeing his favorite ferns again. Christmas ferns were bright green under the trees, and he found a hay-scented fern, and the marginal wood fern, with spores on the margins of the leaves. There were lichens with dimpled centers, called *Umbilicaria*—"If that doesn't look like a bellybutton I don't know what does." Wild mint was about, showy with white blooms. And plenty of bright purple ironweed on the riverbank.

Ed had his pants rolled up, and wore an old pair of running shoes and carried a dip net as we sloshed right into the river—it was only twenty feet across.

I asked him, "What is this green stringy stuff?"

The plant grew in clumps, with tendrils several feet long; you'd see it suspended in the current.

"We just call it riverweed. It has these dense mats with holes inside and there's lots of life hiding in there."

We watched silvery minnows—like tiny airships, fleets of them. They wait in still water, about six inches below the surface—then dash ahead and veer off sharply, still together, as if by telepathic agreement.

The pools are homes for fish and they'll stay close, even when the river is roaring with flash floods. There's a species called the fantail darter that prefers the fast water, living and finding its food right in the rapids. And Ed made a splashing swoop with his net and came up with a black-nose dace. It's about four inches long, gray, with a dark stripe all the way around the nose. I held the fish in my hands. It felt alert and strong.

Many of the fish are in the river because of the insects. In spring the mayfly will hatch and ascend. A trout will see clouds of mayflies rising off the water. Ed said, "An adult mayfly doesn't even have an operational digestive system. They just fly around and mate and lay eggs and die." Unless a trout leaps—in which case they're lunch. Sometimes the mayfly has been tediously crafted by a human and tied to a leader of feathery monofilament—then it's the trout that's threatened.

The mayflies, the caddis flies, the stone flies, spend years in the larval stage. One type of caddis fly will take up a station, say, hidden in the riverweed. Find a home that faces upstream. Spin a silken net that covers the entrance to the hole. The net filters out pieces of leaves or shreds of other insects. The larvae clean the net off and eat the food or else they just eat the whole net and spin another one. Sometimes the larvae will even pull pieces of rock together and spin the web over the crevices.

"They also live under here." Ed pulled up a flat river stone and turned it over. But I couldn't see what he was talking about. "Look, right there. Just a tiny black stone-fly larva." It was barely a spidery smudge on the bottom of the rock. "And there's a caddis fly," Ed said, pushing with his fingernail to make the whitish larva squirm. Some of the larvae will build houses, covering themselves with bits of rock or wood. "You can identify the species by what their houses are made of."

Another rock. Ed said, "There's a stone-fly nymph. In this stage they can get up to two-thirds of an inch long." The black nymph started to run. "There's the two tails, and see, it's got the six legs just like an insect is supposed to have."

The underriver food chain starts at the single-cell level, with algae. Some are called diatoms, and they can be several shades of brown. The diatoms live together in slimy, slippery galaxies—"rock snot," the biologists call them.

The snails love algae and you'll often see a clean path left behind a snail as it eats its way across a rock.

The snails are eaten by the crayfish—muddy brown and up to five inches long. One of Ed Greene's colleagues studies two crayfish species that are found only in the New River.

The crayfish, finally, have to be wary of the great blue heron's long stabbing beak.

We stood for a time in the late afternoon sunlight, listening to the water's dance over rocks. I knew that Ed had a house on the South Fork, downstream from here a few miles.

"Can you always hear the water from your house?"

"Yes, it's just wonderful."

I said, "I've learned already that the best deal is to have a house on flat water, but just below a rapids, so you have the sound to listen to and then a good place to put a boat in."

"That's just what we have—you can sit out on the porch and watch the rapids and listen. A couple of winters back we had the hardest freeze to come along in years and I woke up in the night because all of a sudden it was silent. It was eerie. The river had stopped. That's the only time that's happened."

3

WEAVERS FORD

36° 33'N
81° 22'W

The best driving along the New is slow enough so you can hear the gravel crunching under your tires. My blue single-seat canoe would be on the roof of the Jeep, I'd have the mountain bike and camping gear and a cooler in back. You can follow much of the North Fork through Ashe County by road.

One afternoon I stopped by a farm to ask about a turn that was coming up. An elderly couple was waiting at the road's edge. Their garden lay between the road and the river; the farmhouse and barn were on the hillside above. I asked about directions and complimented the flowers the woman was carrying.

She waved her hand toward the field above the road. "Used to be I had all that in flowers, too, but there comes a time when you have to lay it down."

Her words were soft and rounded, like the edges of an old limestone grave marker.

"Who are *you?*" she soon wanted to know, and after a

while agreed that some of my people could have lived here once, too.

"Well, this is Jess, and I'm Ona, and we've been right here all our lives."

Jess stood behind her, holding a small sledgehammer. He wore green cotton workclothes. His hands were large and lumpy. Ona, I noticed, was wearing high black leather lace-up boots.

I had a sack of peaches just picked the day before and I offered some.

"That's a peach, Jess." She held one in the palm of her hand. And then said to me, quieter, "He's got Alzheimer's. He doesn't recall some things."

Jess had sold plumbing supplies out of High Point for thirty-two years, always coming home weekends to this farm, and the wide porch where he could watch the river. We talked some about North Carolina and what the roads and the towns used to be like, then he slowed, and gazed away.

"Jess is feeling bad," Ona said. "His dog died and he had to bury it. We had him fifteen years."

"What sort of dog was it?"

"Eskimo spitz."

"What was his name?"

"Bear."

Ona moved closer, turning away from Jess. "He took it up on the hill to bury but a neighbor woman went to see and she came to say that he hadn't done a good job and the animals have been getting at it. I don't know if I can tell him or not."

"Do you think you'll get another dog?"

Ona said, "I don't know. Maybe not yet. But it's different without having one. You know, we used to never lock our doors here on the river, with the dog. Now, I do."

4

TODD GENERAL STORE

36° 18′N
81° 36′W

There was woodsmoke in the rainy air on a Sunday as the South Fork Baptist Church was letting out. A new red Ford pickup in the parking lot had a front plate that said: MEAT CAMP VOLUNTEER FIRE DEPARTMENT. Meat Camp is up the valley nearby—it was a mountain outpost for the pioneer hunters.

The storekeeper fixed me a cheese sandwich to take for lunch and I pulled on a rain parka and boots and started out on a nine-mile hike along the river. Until this morning the weather had been dry, and the New's South Fork was running at its lowest level. Troublesome to canoe—some places you'd have to be dragging the boat—and it was better anyway on a chilly day to walk and breathe the water vapor that drifted down the hillsides.

I turned off onto a side road to follow the river to the south, going upstream. My last view of Todd was of the white church steeple above the trees. The churches of the small communities are the *still points* of history—men and women would have stood on the steps of South Fork Baptist talking about what they might do if the North invaded and started the war.

At a driveway there was a yellow and black metal sign with the word DANGER above a drawing of a stick figure man being leaped at by a stick figure dog. I walked on a little faster. A half-mile later a collie and a beagle came scooting out of a yard and into the road, stopping twenty feet away. I'd move on a few steps and they'd advance the same few steps. A yell came from behind a screen door and the dogs looked back. I stamped my foot, "Get on home!" and that amused them. When the dance is at this stage you probably won't get hurt; it's only dogs doing their job. And I've seen them on hot afternoons just too overcome by sunshine to even move off the porch.

The land close by the river seems more comfortable when the weather's wet. At the corner of a fence line I saw a spiderweb's shimmer. The water drops looked like mercury, and the moisture edged the strands of the web. It was a tornado's funnel with steep sides leading down into a hole in the fence post. Inside, where the spider waited, it was dark and timeless.

The river valley—which had been wide enough for some Christmas tree farming—narrowed, and I left the South Fork to follow a road that wound its way up the side of Bald Mountain. As I got higher I was entering the clouds that were hanging off the ridges. Soon I was in steady rain. The drops splashed on the grass and slid across the road in sheets that mixed with mud. A huge, shaggy draft horse watched from the dusk of a barn. Bright green tobacco plants stretched away in rows. A farmhouse in the mist appeared almost neon-purple.

. . .

One side of my family has history in North Carolina. In 1802, Bennett Wellman, his wife, Mary Mulligan, and their eight children crossed Pound Gap into southeastern Kentucky. They had been living in Daniel Boone's territory on the Yadkin River, not far from here, and they could have known Boone, might have followed his enthusiasm. Boone helped open the Wilderness Road, and began leading settlers into Kentucky in 1775.

It was land that had been praised by speculators. Fat, foolish game and soft meadows and uncut forests and yours if you got there early enough. A preacher back east told his congregation, "O my dear honeys, heaven is a Kentucky of a place." But, on one of the early trips, Daniel Boone lost his son James in an Indian attack; the warriors were Delaware, Shawnee, and Cherokee; the boy had been tortured, then killed by ax blows and arrows.

Boone was an explorer and a mountain hunter, leaving his family for a year at a time, hoping to come back with bear meat and venison, and furs. I like to imagine him on winter trapping trips, camping high with his horse and dog. He'd set up a brush shelter and hang a turkey to roast and drip over the fire for his supper. At bedtime he'd settle back with *Gulliver's Travels,* reading about the seafarer's adventure with the tiny people of Lilliput. Captain Gulliver, during his cordial confinement on the island, had—

> ... three hundred cooks to dress my Victuals, with each Goose and Turkey being only a mouthful, along with thimble-sized vials of Liquor.

What could Boone, there by the campfire light, possibly have made of Jonathan Swift's satirical whimseys: that a nation might divide people as to whether they wore low-heeled or high-heeled shoes or commit war over the issue of which end of the egg was to be opened first?

.   .   .

About this same time William Bartram, the naturalist, wrote about his trip into the Carolinas, and described this scene, set in green meadows and strawberry fields, by a meandering river in the mountains:

> ... companies of young, innocent Cherokee virgins, some busy gathering the rich fragrant fruit, others having already filled their baskets, lay reclined under the shade of floriferous and fragrant native bowers of Magnolia, Azalea, Philadelphus, perfumed Calycanthus ... disclosing their beauties to the fluttering breeze, and bathing their limbs in the cool,

fleeting streams; whilst other parties, more gay and libertine, were yet collecting strawberries, or wantonly chasing their companions, tantalising them, staining their lips and cheeks with the rich fruit.

The Cherokee were the mountain Indians. Intelligent, gentle, fierce. And angered when the Scots-Irish and the German and English settlers pushed into the southern Appalachians, hunting and trapping. The Indians were incredulous to learn that the whites actually wanted to *own* the land.

It was thought the Cherokee Nation might become part of America. But in 1829 a gold rush ripped into Cherokee Territory in north Georgia. The legislature of that state passed a law against Indians digging for gold. The lawmakers also said the Cherokee could move west, to a place of their own in what would become Oklahoma. They could take their slaves along for farming. The question was debated and negotiated for years. Several thousand Cherokee went ahead, voluntarily—it was a nine-hundred-mile journey.

In May 1838 the U.S. Army *enforced* the migration. Fifteen thousand Cherokee this time, and many of their black slaves. They were captured and put on wagons, put on boats, made to walk, exhausted, often barefoot, the old and the very young dying from cholera and fevers and whooping cough. The heaps of dirt on the graves marked what the Cherokee called the Trail Where They Wept.

On summer evenings in the town of Cherokee, down on the eastern edge of the Great Smoky Mountains, the outdoor drama *Unto These Hills* portrays these events. It is romantic musical history with an upbeat ending. Many in the cast are Eastern Cherokee—some are descendants of those who managed to hide in the high coves. It's disconcerting, at first, to hear the soft Appalachian accents of the young Cherokee men helping park cars outside the amphitheater where their story is told.

.   .   .

My walk brought me out of the raincloud and down to the South Fork. Then the road followed an old railroad grade, running upstream along the river, back into Todd. I picked up my pace and I'd smile and nod at every car that came along. There'd be a friendly lift of a finger from the steering wheel. Once a fellow in a pickup going the other way looked up in his rearview mirror and waved.

Might be a relative, way back.

5

STATE HIGHWAY 221

36° 28'N
81° 20'W

A day's canoe trip starts in a panicky buzz that changes in a moment to a sweet, susurrant glide.

Don't lock the keys in the Jeep! Try to get the canoe down off the racks and over to the river's edge without banging it around. Be sure you have your water bottles. And your watch and the sunglasses and sunscreen and a hat and a bandanna in case you lose the hat. Tie a spare paddle up under the thwarts.

Other canoe voyagers were close to departing, on this sloping bank of the South Fork—an outfitter's put-in, just below the 221 bridge. A young father in swim trunks walked out into the shallow water, pulling along the rental canoe that already carried his wife and two small children; he'd have a tricky move getting himself into the boat. A teenager was fitting a cooler into a canoe, and whistling; it took a moment before I recognized the music from *Deliverance*—a movie that came out several years before he was born.

I eased my canoe down off the bank and kept a hand on it as it trembled in the water. The river was cold, a murky green under the clouds. A dripping step over the gunwale and I settled in, kneeling, with my back against the center thwart.

The boat rocked, then steadied, and the current caught the bow and turned it downstream. Then a touch with the paddle to add some speed. This is the moment of grace. There is a hushed rippling as the water carries you away and you feel as if you could look back at the bank and see yourself as a faint tracing in the air.

The canoe is a fourteen-foot Mohawk. My paddle is an old wooden bent-shaft, splintering at the blade's edge—it's not intended for the rocky work of eastern rivers. I reached out for a few guiding strokes, to bring the boat to the center of the current. Then I used a deeper pull to swing the bow clear of a sudden, black rock. When the sky is overcast it's hard to see the rocks that surface just a few inches above the water, and the bigger ones can spin you sideways, kicking your pulse rate up as you fight to keep the upstream rail from going under.

This is a kindly stretch of river, though, early on. It's only Class I rapids, whitewater splashing past rocks and pouring across ledges. Sometimes in smooth water the bottom of the canoe will flex over an algae-slicked underwater shelf—it's as if you're crossing the back of an ancient furry creature that could, if angered, rise up dripping and groaning.

I tried to be a river animal once. It was after a sticky, hot night and I'd been camping along the South Fork. When the sun started to slant down into the valley I decided it was time to get wet. I had been fearful of the water, concerned about flipping the canoe, too mistrustful of the river's darker parts.

But on this morning I waded in and let the coolness travel up my legs. Then a gasping dunk so I could taste the water and hear the current burble past my ears. I pointed my feet downstream and floated—from rock, to ledge, to pool. I could turn around and kneel in the water and hold my chest against the flow. At this level I could see the New River coming around a slow bend and then *downhill* to me. I was looking at perhaps a one-foot drop. The New loses 3,216 feet in elevation from Snake Mountain down to its end in West Virginia.

Back at the outfitter's this morning I'd asked about this section of the river. (There are six classes of whitewater. A Class V rapids could be treacherous even for expert paddlers. A Class VI is simply ultra-extreme.)

"Any Class IIIs down there?"

"Nah, and there's just one II; it's a few miles down. It's a good ride—just remember to stay left and you'll be fine."

I was happy about this. I wouldn't want to try a Class III rapids by myself. Even a Class II—I began to think as I came around a bend and saw it coming up—could be more fun than I wanted. As you approach, you *hear* the rapids more than you see them, because of the drop in the landscape. But I could spot a distinct line across the river, huge boulders on the right side, water spray on the left.

The noise grew louder. The water seemed flatter in the middle, coming into a V, and I started to go that way thinking the outfitter was wrong, but a stronger current pulled me away and to the left, down through a chute between two rocks, and I had to reach far out with the paddle for a sweep stroke to draw the bow back to the right for a drop over a three-foot ledge.

My little canoe likes to turn back upstream after it goes through rapids—you have to work a bit to straighten it out. But this time I let the boat come on around so I could see this Class II from the downriver side. The tempting route through the middle was an easy drop over a ledge, but a drop directly *onto* a pile of nasty rocks. The outfitter's "left" advice had been right. But I wondered if this rapids didn't have a touch of Class III, because you had to maneuver some and the correct line wasn't obvious.

The boat slowed into a long pool, with the water reflecting calm from bank to bank. I laid the paddle across the gunwales and poured coffee from the Thermos. There was no apparent current. Then a white duck's feather overtook the boat on the right, its curve catching the downstream breeze. Whirligig waterbugs—their feet dimpling the surface tension—winked about in parallel zigs and zags.

It is mostly farming country here. There are a few fishing camps, cabins, and small trailers close to the bank. If you have been lucky enough to buy some land on a hillside above the river, and sensible, you will build of natural materials and situate the house so it's tucked away and facing downstream—a canoeist would have to look over his shoulder, back up the valley, to see it. If you put your summer home in full view of the river, and use an enthusiastic color of paint, the local people will say you have a "Florida house."

I stopped for lunch at a low-water bridge. Had to pull the boat out anyway to carry it across the road; the river level was just two feet below the concrete span. In springtime rains this bridge would be awash and dangerous even for a car.

The early afternoon brightened and warmed and I drifted the last few miles down the South Fork, almost sleeping past the small rapids. I watched a family of ducks doing whitewater maneuvers—"ferrying" at an angle against the current so as to cross the river in a straight line. You can follow ducks down through the rapids; they aim for the V and tilt easily over the dropoffs.

Some large white cattle had come down close to the water. They were dozing and blinking on the sandy bank under the willow trees and one seemed close to tumbling in. The sunlight was sparkling up the shallow river and I was thinking this was the prettiest spot I'd seen—when I noticed *another* river coming in from the left. I had arrived at the spot where the North Fork meets the South, and the day's trip was over.

But I wasn't ready and I spun around to paddle back upstream for a while. It was easy going against the slight current, and I could stop and hold the boat motionless; then watch the slow turn of the bow, moving downriver.

6

_____

THE CONFLUENCE

36° 32'N
81° 21'W

The shuttle truck came along pretty close to the pickup time. I had the canoe waiting by the road, and Chris, the driver, flipped it up and tied it down.

"Good day, huh?" he grinned, knowing that while working *close* to the river might be satisfying, being *on* the river is a whole lot better.

"Yeah," I said. "Thought I was going to get wet twice, though. Once with the rain but that didn't come—then I figured I might be swimming out of that Class II back there."

"That's a fine one," said Chris. "You know, there's a private road that goes in there but we know the guy and a lot of times we'll take kayaks down and just play."

We were driving back to the outfitter's and sometimes the road would run along next to the river. Chris was keeping track of the rental canoes that were still out, and we pulled over when he spotted a family having lunch on the riverbank.

"They'll never make their pickup time," he told me, climbing back in the truck. "They're not halfway yet, been having trouble. They've flipped twice."

Chris had convinced the family to aim for a different take-out point, one within a couple of hours' reach. The company tries to have all the boats off the water by 5:30.

He said, "You can get a few who don't understand about the river at all. We've had people come up here who think somehow that it goes around in a circle—that you would get out at the same place you put in. It's hard to figure out what sort of picture they have in their minds."

Chris works construction during the week, and weekends for the canoe outfitter. When November comes and the river business stops, he'll work "in the Christmas trees" on Saturdays and Sundays, helping with the harvesting and wreath making. Then in the really cold months it's up to the mountains for a ski resort job. It's close to a year-round seven-day week.

When we pulled into the outfitter's yard there was a charcoal grill going for hamburgers—suppertime for the crew. The canoe racks were filling back up; some of the more seasoned boats were scabrous with fiberglass patches, in yellow and green and gray, on the red and green hulls. I noticed a few new scrapes on the side of my own canoe.

Chris said he *does* manage to get on the river on some of these weekends. He'll take a boat and borrow a ride to the state park several miles upstream. Put up his tent on the grass there and after breakfast in the morning it's a great cruise into work.

.   .   .

Several river outfitters have told me the two big pushes for canoeing and rafting came from the 1972 Summer Olympics in Munich, where whitewater events were held for the first time, and from the movie *Deliverance*.

It was director John Boorman's picture, James Dickey's novel. Dickey was a successful poet, enthralled with the notion of celebrity. He'd roll into a college town and slur his way through an often glorious reading. Later there'd be more drinking at the reception, and pliant young women. People who saw him would talk about it years later. James Dickey intended his first novel to make him even more famous.

Deliverance was a bestseller in the summer of 1970. It is the story of four men from the Atlanta suburbs and their canoe trip down a river—fictionally the Cahulawasee—through the mountains in Georgia's northeast corner. There is death on the river, and rape.

The book's dust jacket is black with green lettering. And a green circle at the top, with dark leaves and a single, blue eye—staring. The men in the canoes on the Cahulawasee are inexperienced and frightened of the water. And there's a darker apprehension of the woods and the mountain people.

On the second day of the trip Dickey's narrator is starting to relax in the boat:

> . . . the river seemed to go deeper and deeper under us; the colors changed toward denser greens as the sun got higher. The pace of the water began to pick

up; we slid farther and farther with each stroke. I thought to myself that anyone fighting the brush along the bank could not keep up with us.

Then in the turn of a page: "Two men stepped out of the woods, one of them trailing a shotgun by the barrel."

The riverbank rape follows. And it is the movie version of this scene that plays in our minds. We see Jon Voight tied to a tree, with a knife at his neck. Ned Beatty, pale and quivering, taking off his shirt and pants.

"Them panties too," the mountain man says, in both movie and book. But only on the screen is Ned Beatty's character forced to squeal like a pig, the mountain man riding his back, twisting his ear.

Jon Voight is next. He is pushed to his knees. The other man starts to unbutton his pants, handing the shotgun to his friend. Then—an arrow appears in his buddy's chest. As Dickey writes:

> . . . a foot and a half of bright red arrow was shoved forward from the middle of his chest. It was so suddenly there it seemed to have come from within him.

The audience knows that Lewis had to have shot the arrow; Lewis the survivalist, played by Burt Reynolds. He had been following in the second canoe.

The other mountain man gets away. The men from the

city decide not to tell what happened, to bury the body in the woods. There is more mayhem to come.

Christopher Dickey, James Dickey's son, worked with the movie crew during the location filming of *Deliverance,* in Rabun County, Georgia. He was Ned Beatty's stand-in for the rape scene. He liked Beatty, whose background was stage acting, and who had come to Georgia following the run of an Ionesco play. But Ned Beatty's mood changed during the filming of the rape. And so did Christopher Dickey's, as he describes in his 1998 memoir, *Summer of Deliverance:*

> That night I called my father. I was sick of the film, sick of the whole story. And I wondered why the hell he had to have this homosexual rape. "I had to put the moral weight of murder on the suburbanites," was what my father told me. It was what he always said . . . I don't think my father understood what had happened that day filming by the river. In the book you can read the rape scene and know it happened, but you get around it and go on, and get other things out of the novel. In the movie—it was becoming what the movie was about, it was the thing everybody was going to remember.

When Christopher Dickey's book came out I talked with him about his father's experience in the north Georgia mountains, if there had been logic behind the sodomy scene. He said, "I don't think it's endemic of

Appalachia but I do think it's not uncommon in a certain society of violent men . . . for all you know these are escaped prisoners. I don't think you can generalize from it that it goes on all the time but that wasn't the point."

I said, "Your father saw it as a metaphor?"

"Well, yes. And there's also throughout his work, as many scholars and people have remarked, a kind of homoerotic quality. He was fascinated by men and the company of men, principally in sports but also in war. He wanted to make a film about Sparta, for instance, and I think he wanted to make it basically because he read a line in some poetry by Robert Lowell talking about the Spartans combing out one another's 'golden Botticellian hair' before the battle of Thermopylae."

I have always been more haunted by an earlier scene in *Deliverance*. The men from Atlanta drive up to a gas station on a ridge above the river. No one's around, and Jon Voight walks up on the porch of a cabin, out back. He looks in through the screen door and sees an old woman and a retarded child. It is a glimpse for horrific effect. And it is John Boorman's touch, not James Dickey's.

It is hard to know how much damage was done by the images in the film. I've met many people who are afraid of Appalachia. I've heard of a couple from New York City, visiting friends in North Carolina, who panicked at the suggestion of a day trip over into West Virginia. "We don't want to go anywhere close to that state."

7

SHATLEY SPRINGS

36° 28'N
81° 24'W

I smell ham," the man said, getting out of his car and hitching up his pants. He and his wife arrived with another couple—the men riding in front, the women in the backseat. They parked next to me on the grass. It was the aroma of *country* ham in the air.

The dining was family-style—sit down with happy strangers. One of them said, "I tried not to eat all day," and started passing the platters: fried chicken and piled-high slivers of dark, salty ham. Mashed potatoes and brown gravy and green beans and fried apples and slaw and biscuits. Young women and men waiting to pour iced tea and coffee and bring ice cream or pie or cobbler. You have to remember to sit up straight and take slow breaths.

This is the Shatley Springs Inn: a low, aged wooden building painted dark red with green trim; a restaurant and a gift shop, white rockers on the porch, a pavilion for music, and eleven red cottages arranged alongside a good-sized fishing pond.

At the far end of the porch, just as the Shatley Springs brochure reads: "The spring itself is always running and the water is free."

The water comes out of a steel pipe, slightly below ground level; you walk down concrete steps to stand and fill your bottles. The water that isn't carried away flows out into the pond and then spills into a creek on its way to the New's North Fork.

One of the water gatherers had driven thirty miles up from Wilkesboro. He had enough gallon jugs to put a good weight in the back of his truck. He said, "I've been getting water here since 1937. I even come in the wintertime when they're closed."

The water comes cold from deep under Little Phoenix Mountain and has a reputation for healing. It carries traces of ammonium chloride, sodium chloride, sodium sulphate, sodium nitrate, calcium bicarbonate, iron, magnesium, silica, and alumina. The brochure claims:

> On a summer day in 1890, Martin Shatley was passing by a mountain stream and paused to dip his hands and face in the water to soothe his hot, blistered skin. Only a few hours later he discovered that the crippling skin disease which had plagued him for many years seemed to be miraculously disappearing.

Mr. Shatley wrote about his affliction—the swelling and burning and plagues of boils. And a bad cough and a bleeding of his right lung. Five of the best physicians "never could do me any good." After he found the water, he said, "I was so glad I felt like shouting; I was glad with all my heart." And thirty-five years later: "I have done as much hard work since that time as any man I know of."

After supper I filled a couple of half-gallon jugs for myself, and left while there was still good light. It was a chance to explore the roads winding through the narrow valleys down to the North Fork. But I stopped at the first farm on past Shatley Springs.

I'd noticed a sign: GLADS $5. Turned out to be five dollars a dozen for the tall flower stalks—red and magenta and yellow and white and salmon—spiking up out of the red tilled earth in a patch near the kitchen door.

The owners came out to help. Eddie had a short, curved knife and I'd point and he'd bend and cut close to the ground. His wife, Betty, brought some white plastic pails, half-full of water, and we made a secure place for the glads in the back of the Jeep.

"How many do you have growing?" I asked.

Betty said, "We put in twenty thousand gladiola bulbs every spring. The deer get a lot of them." There were a few strands of wire running from post to post around the flowers.

They farmed corn and raised tobacco and had some Fraser firs growing on the mountain. "The Christmas trees take a lot of work," Eddie told me. "I've just had a crew up there today, trimming, you know." I'd noticed three young Hispanic men, leaving in a pickup with Texas plates.

"Those fellows from out of state?" I asked.

Eddie said, "You know, it's hard to get help anymore from around here. But these fellows show up ready to work, and they're good. They get the job done."

8

JEFFERSON PEAK

36° 24'N
81° 27'W

Stand at the top of Mount Jefferson, at 4,683 feet, and you'll see the Ashe County Christmas trees, arrayed in dark evergreen smudges on the hills below. John Fraser, a Scotsman from London, one of the early botanizers, found the high-altitude fir. Of course the Cherokee knew the tree, and the white settlers called it "she-balsam"—they would drain the resin from breastlike blisters on the bark, to use in tanning leather.

The Fraser thrives now in cultivation, but is perishing at the highest elevations. A month earlier in an almost snowy fog I had turned off the Blue Ridge Parkway to drive the road up Mount Mitchell, then walked the path to the summit, the very top of the Appalachian range. The Fraser firs lay bleached and scattered, thousands of trees felled by an insect: the balsam woolly adelgid. Acid rain also hurts, souring the clouds that swirl over the high peaks—it's practically lemon-juice air.

On the older maps of western North Carolina, Jefferson

Peak is called Nigger Mountain. A sign at a viewpoint up on the parkway says it was known as Negro Mountain. There's talk about escaped slaves having hidden in the caves below, but the name probably comes from the outcroppings of black rock near the summit, especially visible in winter.

You can get a good sense of how the New River lays from the overlooks on Mount Jefferson. The South Fork flows in loops through the farmland to the east. You can't see the North Fork but you can follow the lines of its sheltering mountains—Three Top Mountain, then Phoenix and Little Phoenix. And the map names the creeks that tumble and cut and suggest stories of wildlife and settlers: Sugar Branch, Little Horse, Bear, Dog, Roan, Cox, Endicott, Halsey, Morgan, Gambill, Cobb.

I watched the cloud shadows passing across the ridges, seeming to bend as they folded down into the valleys. There are people in the coves below who know that the *Phoenix* was an immigrant ship that brought Germans to port in Philadelphia. The Eller family was on that crossing, and there's an Eller cemetery here, close to the North Fork.

. . .

I've spent long afternoons in the Ashe County Library, looking in vain for evidence that some of my family might have settled here. In past research I've placed my father's forebears—Arthur and Peggy Adams—in eastern

Kentucky. They show up on the 1850 state census. It's thought they came from Virginia, but as one genealogist put it, "Arthur was too young to have established any legal trail before he arrived in Kentucky." The Adams name can be English or Irish, and, in past travels, I've felt very much at home in Dublin, and especially in Northern Ireland. Ulster Protestants, these Adamses would be: I've almost seen myself walking down the street in Belfast.

My mother's family name is Wellman, and I was having trouble tracing them back *out* of Kentucky as well. Then late one night it occurred to me to try the Internet. I searched for the name and within seconds opened The Wellman Family History Page. Albert Wellman, a distant cousin in North Carolina, had collected the genealogy and was adding to it as fast as Wellmans around the world happened onto the site. I had no idea that all these kinfolk existed, including my far-off cousin.

It was Thomas Wellman most of us were looking for, the man who had come to Massachusetts from England in about 1645, beginning the American family line that can be followed to Maryland, to North Carolina, into Kentucky, and to my mother: Edith Lona Wellman. I phoned Albert down in Durham; he told me that no one he knew of had been to Ilminster, Thomas's birthplace. And so after the cold weather came and I had left the New River, I flew to London, then took a train from Paddington Station out to the West Country to Somerset County.

Ilminster is a comfortable place with cottages and row houses, a narrow shopping street with the bank and the butcher's and a bakery. And the Minster itself, the grand honey-colored stone church built around 1450.

Fifteen minutes after I arrived in town I was talking with Barry Wellman. We were both surprised. There were only a few Wellmans listed in the Somerset County phone books but the hotel desk clerk said, "Sure I know one, right down the street." And when I showed up and explained myself, Barry and his wife, Denise, couldn't stop saying, "Cor." They said it softly in a wondering breath. (I didn't know then that the word is a variant of "God," and quite useful depending on how strongly you say it.) To be sure, here was a relative come from the States, but it was the resemblance that had us laughing. Barry was about forty, and he had light brown hair and blue eyes, a complexion with hints of red and a familiar long, thin nose. That describes several million Englishmen but he sure looked like the Wellman pictures I'd grown up seeing.

In the early years the people of England had single names. But if in a parish there were two Johns, the fellow who made the bread would be John the Baker, and the one with the sheep would be John the Shepherd. John De Winterhay had lived in town and I'd noticed a sign along the street for Winterhay Meadow. Also: a Miller, a Broome, a Gardener, a King, and a Corporal Lanceworthy of the Royal Fusillers. Our Thomas Wellman, I assume, had an ancestor who lived by a good source of water.

The archives had mention of Wellmans paying tithes to the Ilminster church. And on a Sunday night I sat in a back pew at Evensong service, trying to place Thomas there beside me. The voices of the choir rose under the high ceilings; even a breath seemed to echo. It would have been much darker in the church, long ago, with only the smoky candles for light. Parishioners had been entombed in the walls, under the floor, and outside in the moss-covered ground, haphazardly double and triple buried.

It's known that Thomas volunteered in the English Civil War, to help Parliament chase down the rebels who were demanding religious freedom. It's said he fought alongside a young friend who'd already been to Massachusetts and that after the war they left to go back there together.

"But," I asked at the local pub, the Crown, "how would Thomas Wellman, this young man from Ilminster, probably from a family of tradesmen, decide to go off to such a wild place as America?"

"Ah, but the lads loved the countryside. Even now there's lots of hunting around—though it's mostly not legal." This happened to be the butcher speaking and I'd seen venison, boar, and partridge in his shop window. He said, "Sometimes here in the pub you'll see money change hands for a bin bag of pheasants under the table."

Ilminster slept that night under the deepest blue sky with a scrim of fog and coal smoke above the homes in the valley. And I wondered how long the knowledge of this place remained with the Wellmans of America. Did Thomas tell his children stories of England? Did Bennett Wellman, Thomas's great-grandson, crossing the Appalachian range into Kentucky, ever have the slightest thought of Ilminster?

9

MOUTH OF WILSON

36° 35'N
81° 20'W

How high would the water have come up?" I asked the man behind the counter at the gas station and garage and farm supply store in the community named for the good-sized stream that joins the New from the west. Wilson Creek picks up the flow from its own final tributaries, Bear Branch and Trout Branch, and rolls on into the river. That would be the "mouth" of Wilson, the point at which the creek enters the larger stream.

"That lake would have been over the top of your head, right where you're standing," he explained. And he was looking several feet above my head to some point out in the air. That meant the old white house on the hillside across the road would have been covered, and the small elderly woman whose image I'd seen behind her lace curtains would have had to leave.

"Mouth of Wilson was going under, no doubt about it," he said. "My dad was one of those who fought it hard, and they won."

The dam that had been proposed for this stretch of the New River, a few decades ago, was a big project. A power company would buy the farms, move the families, and provide cheap electricity for progress somewhere else. They'd leave a lake behind the dam for water skiing. Beneath the water—houses, churches, and twelve cemeteries.

I'd been to church in the morning and I was thinking about baptism, and the belief of some denominations that to be truly reborn you must be immersed in moving water.

The deacons of the New River Missionary Baptist Church were smiling at the door, and when the time came I stood up from my pew in the back and said my name and where I was from. We'd been given a church bulletin with announcements, about Bible study meeting and a baby shower. And this Sunday's prayer list: including Tammy's Dad & Sister, Macajune Blackburn, Donna's Grandmother, Pauline Shatley Family, Debbie's Mother, and Lost Family Members. The minister led prayers for the people on the list, and one was offered for all the Lost, plus the church members who were away traveling. Several in the congregation raised their hands to add a prayer request or report that a relative was doing better and soon should be coming home from the hospital.

The sermon was skipped today because the Vacation Bible School kids would be showing off what they'd learned: poems and tiny essays and a beaver puppet performing in a funny skit with the preacher.

There was no mention of baptism during the service, and in the parking lot afterwards a member explained that if someone had been saved and was ready to join the church, they'd all meet down at the river, usually after Sunday dinner.

·   ·   ·

That afternoon, though, farther along the river, I did find a baptism service.

The New runs straight north to cross the state line into Virginia, then, at Mouth of Wilson, loops sharply to the east and widens out. Here it becomes recreational, with camping trailer parks and lots of family boating. But I have seen the water in this section in early spring running angry and muddy, and when I stopped today to talk with a man who lived directly across the road from a wide stretch, he said, "Sure, it's a dangerous river. People have drowned right out there."

As I drove around a loop of the river I saw some people gathered at the water's edge. I pulled over and drove down to a public launching site: a dirt parking lot and a sloping boat ramp. There was a tall man standing with his back to the water. About twenty-five people were assembled in a half-circle around him. I left the Jeep back under the trees and slowly walked up close to the group.

The preacher was wearing a white shirt, buttoned at the neck and wrists, and dress pants. His steel-colored hair was combed in ridges. He had a Bible, closed, laid on his left palm. He would gesture with the other hand and then bring it flat to rest on the top of the Bible.

Two people left the group to stand at the preacher's side—a woman and her son. He looked to be in his early twenties. They were both wearing T-shirts and shorts. The preacher said they were making this profession of faith together, to renew their lives.

He led them into the river, which was green and swirling in a quiet eddy; we were just upstream from a sandbar. Two of the church men were helping; they would stand behind the mother and son, to ease them into the water and lift them back up.

A prayer was spoken, and the words: "I baptize thee in the name of the Father and Son and Holy Ghost."

The mother crossed her arms over her chest, reaching a hand up to hold her nose shut. The preacher placed his right hand behind her neck and laid her slowly backwards. For a moment she was all the way under the surface of the water. Then she rose, with a gasp for air. She accepted a towel. Her son stood straighter, and grim, awaiting his turn.

When it was over and everyone was laughing and dripping, the preacher gathered his riverbank congregation into a circle, holding hands. They sang "Amazing Grace." Some had their eyes shut, praying. Some were looking directly at the sky.

The preacher said, "Is there anybody else while I've got my baptizing shoes on?" His question seemed directed at an older woman who had a pained expression, but he smiled for a moment's pause and didn't push.

"I tell people all the time not to go on about how cold the water is," the preacher said as we talked some afterwards. "You don't want to be discouraging if someone's thinking about it."

"What happens in the wintertime?" I asked.

"There's a baptism font at another church nearby that we borrow but it's slippery in there, they don't take care of it. This is better, the river. And it's where everybody can see it. A baptism is the public profession of faith."

Some of the church members asked me if I'd like to come to their singing service that night and I wrote down the directions, but I drove on east along the river road and by evening was too far away to return.

. . .

A couple of days earlier, back on the South Fork, I had canoed past the collapsed timbers and orphaned apple trees of a nineteenth-century homestead. In the water along the bank there was an old rotted flatboat; you wouldn't even step into it now. In the old days people would use a boat like this to cross the river, to where there *was* a road. Maybe they'd even keep a Model-T on the other side. You can imagine a Sunday-morning scene in vague-focus pastel: the gentleman of the farm, and his wife, getting into the boat. He's wearing his black suit and the stiff collar that folds over the tie. She's in a ruffly white-fronted long dress and wearing a hat. She's raised her skirts out of the mud and taken her place on the plank seat, holding her purse. He'd step in quickly, judging the speed of the current as he pushes off with a long chestnut pole. He'd stand at the stern and lean over hard, poling the flatboat at an upriver angle so as to arrive at a point directly across from the farm.

10

FRIES MILL

36° 42′N
80° 59′w

You can see the past century of Fries, Virginia, as you come around the turn on Route 94 and start down the hill into town: the New River pooling behind a slanting dam, redbrick abandoned factory buildings, a main street with two blocks of businesses, a school, churches, and small white houses on the hillside leading up from the river and the railroad tracks.

The textile baron who gave the town his name pronounced it "freeze" and the preference is honored, although people wait for a chance to grin and tell you, "It's *freeze* in the wintertime and *fries* in the summer."

Mr. Fries was from North Carolina, where he had some textile mills, and this little New River valley seemed ideal for another one. Use the river for power, get a train line going. Roll in the bales of cotton and roll out the bales of cloth. The mill operated until the fall of 1988.

A historical marker tells the story of the New River

Train Song, a standard of old-time music and bluegrass. The Norfolk and Western system had a line that originated here and ran down along the river for fifty miles. "Ridin' on That New River Train," the sign tells me, was one of the early country-music songs recorded—in the 1920s—by Henry Whitter, Kelly Harrell, and E. V. Stoneman (I remember Pop Stoneman and his family band from a Saturday afternoon TV show). All three men lived in Fries and worked in the mill.

I wandered around among the empty buildings, trying to hear the heyday sounds of a mill at full pitch. Whines and grinding squeals and clattering, instead of the crickets in the hot midmorning. And the chuffs of the steam engines backing freight cars along the siding.

"The company at one time owned the town—everything," a man in a khaki shirt and jeans told me as we talked out in front of a cafe. "The drugstore, the hardware stores, furniture store, men's and ladies' clothing."

"Did they use scrip?"

"Sure. If you ran out of money you could go to the paymaster and get scrip against what you had coming. There was coin scrip too. It's collector prices on all that now."

Winfrey Johnson went on to tell me his family's history in the mill. His grandfather had been a loom mechanic, his father ran a knotter. Winfrey started working four hours a day during his high school senior year. He'd wanted a chance at a football varsity letter but his dad said he couldn't support him anymore and it was time to earn his way. He was in and out of the mill for most of twenty years. Dangerous work; lots of men around town now with incomplete hands. "That one guy, I had to take him to the hospital; the carding machine ate his fingers off."

We spoke about the Old Fiddler's Convention, starting up that evening in Galax, fifteen miles away. Winfrey Johnson had never been; Fries would be having its own old-time festival the following weekend. "I was born and raised in bluegrass," he said. "My uncle played mandolin and I spent many a Saturday night up there burning hot dogs over an outside fire just listening to the music."

I walked on through town to a small park and ball field set close to the river. There was a shiny reddish orange N & W caboose—now a town information center—sitting up proudly on its last section of track: WELCOME TO FRIES: WHERE THE TRAIL BEGINS. The empty track bed by the river is now a bike and hiking trail.

A woman on a nearby front porch helped me identify a pink-blossomed vine among the spray of flowers I'd collected. "Would you know the name of this?" I asked, holding it up so she could see. "That's sweet pea," she said, and of course it was but I'd never seen it growing wild.

"You've got goldenrod there, and those white ones are chigger flowers. Queen Anne's Lace is what the name is really. You can take the big ones like that and lay them on wax paper and spray them with hair spray and they won't crumble when they dry. They stay pretty and white and people put them on Christmas trees."

She wasn't planning on going to the Fiddler's Convention either. She said, "It's not Christian. When I was saved I turned and started in the other direction. I can't see Jesus going over there in a crowd like that where they drink and do all sort of things. When I was a teenager I thought there was nothing like that country music, but it don't give glory to God."

She had worked in the Fries textile mill for fifteen years when she was young, then moved to Indiana. This was a back-home visit with her brother and his friends. She said, "They're pretty musical," and I suspected they'd be spending their evenings over in Galax.

11

GALAX TOWN

36° 39'N
80° 54'W

Galax is named for the southern Appalachian wildflower *Galax urceolata*. The notion of it brings to mind the Carter Family song "Wildwood Flower." It has a tall center stem of white blossoms, but it's the leaf that brings in money. Galax leaves are lustrous and heart-shaped and stay green in flower arrangements. People walk out of the woods with burlap bags full of the stuff.

The town of Galax spreads out in a valley that has Chestnut Creek at its center. A Norfolk & Western branch once ran north out of Galax along Chestnut Creek to join up with the main line at the New River.

I had bean-and-cheese burritos in a Mexican restaurant and drove to the town park for the Fiddler's Convention's first evening, thankful that I'd made my motel reservation a month ago.

It was five dollars to leave the car in someone's front yard and five dollars to get through the front gate and join the thousands already listening to music. I went down the hill into a swirl of dust and the smell of burned popcorn and Polish sausage. At a Good Samaritan booth the First Baptist Church offered cups of water and coffee. A local bank had pulled in a trailer with two ATMs and people were lined up for cash. You could buy T-shirts, baseball caps, CDs, cassettes, vinyl, eight-track tapes. Or invest in an instrument and start your own legend; one banjo maker offered his regular model plus open-back banjos, guitar-banjos, and piccolo-banjos.

The PA sound was ringing from the stage: the opening night is for solo players: Old-time Fiddle, Mandolin, Autoharp, Clawhammer Banjo, and Dobro. Old men, teenage girls, four-foot-high children, and guys who work as accountants in Roanoke or in furniture in High Point. They walk briskly out and kick off a standard tune like "Whistlin' Rufus" and then vanish through the backstage door. Some are very special, shy musicians, and some just grin at their own mishaps. To enter the competition you have to pay the fee and be able to play "a recognizable verse and chorus."

"This is the hardest damn music there is to play," I heard a guitarist say as I passed by a half-circle of lawn chairs under an awning stretched out from a camper. "I used to play in a rhythm and blues outfit in Illinois and this is the hardest damn music to play."

My visit was on Wednesday—the campers had pulled into the park early Sunday morning. There were hundreds of RVs and pickups with trailers or shells. They'd been waiting out on the street for Saturday night to pass and the gates to open so they could try to get a better spot than they had last year.

But the Muddy Creek Band bus came two days later and still got a good place. One of the musicians in a lawn chair out front told me: "They always save a place for us here on this first row 'cause they like the way this bus looks, I guess. We've been right here for eighteen years."

The '55 Chevy bus was a resplendent blue with the band's name on the side in big white letters. The first time the Muddy Creek Band came up from North Carolina they camped in a tent and "liked to drowned." So they bought the bus they'd seen out behind a church—wrote a check for three hundred dollars and put in a new battery and plugs and points. At home they play two or three times a week, different places around the county.

I asked, "What's your instrument?"

"Mandolin. We do a combination bluegrass and old country. We can play probably for five hours and never play the same song twice unless it's asked for."

He said he worked in the Stroh's brewery in Winston-Salem, had been there twenty-eight years. He and all the band members lived in some proximity to Muddy Creek.

"Do you ever sing 'Rank Strangers'?" I asked, about my favorite Stanley Brothers song.

"Sometimes we do. You gotta be in good voice to do that."

"Who's your mandolin hero?" I asked.

"John Duffy of The Seldom Scene. Nobody would play like Duffy. Bill Monroe, he's *everybody's* hero, and Sonny

Osborne plays good but he don't take as many lead breaks like he used to so I guess arthritis is getting to him, but I love John Duffy. He's hard driving. He plays like he's *killing* it. And he was the same man from the first time I saw him in '66 or '67."

He was talking about Duffy's crew cut and blustery bowling-shirt style, and probably that he never quit smoking before he died of a heart attack.

I said, "It was too bad we lost him this year. And Bill Monroe too, although he was a lot older."

He shook his head. "My doctor talked to me about smoking and drinking. He said quit. Liked to cut my damn throat. You get to where you can't do nothing but go to work and go home and eat and go to bed. What's left?"

Down the next row of campers I stopped to ask a young woman about a handsome old fiddle. She was also from North Carolina.

"I found it in pieces in this antique store. It's German. It was made in 1796, but it was in three pieces in a box marked twenty dollars. I took it to a fellow to have it put together so I could hang it up and he said, 'You're not going to put this one on the wall.' "

It turned out to be a fine instrument and she would play it this night on the competitor's stage. Back home, she told me, she works with people who are handicapped, trains them to use service dogs. Last year her brother insisted she come with him to the Galax festival.

"He brought me up here because I was so stressed out, it

was the lowest point for me. But I heard my first bluegrass song here one year ago; I had never heard bluegrass before in my life. Now I've got a permanent callus on my neck from having that thing up against my neck hours a day."

Long moments went by as she held her fiddle. As if waiting to join in a tune.

"It's hard to explain it," she said, looking down. "When you're playing sometimes there's chills up your back."

·　·　·

I followed the gospel notes of a guitar and ended up under a blue tarp along the side of a small RV. A man had the guitar and the lead, and two women, just singing, one watching his face, the other with eyes shut, came into the harmony:

> *Drifting too far from shore, peaceful shore*
> *Come to Jesus today, let him show you the way,*
> *You're drifting too far from the shore.*

Then the man said softly, "One more time," and they sang the chorus again above the deep rhythm of the guitar.

·　·　·

A young man walked by carrying a mandolin, a guitar in a case with an Amnesty International sticker, and a lawn chair. You'll also see bass players with their instruments on two-wheeled carts. *The Gazette,* the Galax newspaper, had published some guidelines for jam sessions at the convention. Including, THOU SHALT COMMUNICATE WHO HAS THE SOLO: "When handing off an instrumental break, follow a pattern, like clockwise around a circle, so the next lead player knows it is his/her turn. If the lead player passes, he/she can indicate with a shake of their head." Also, THOU SHALT NOT RAID: "Do not interrupt an active jam by calling favorite musicians away to begin another jam. After a reasonable amount of time, any jam session will change musicians."

.   .   .

I went back to the motel about ten o'clock, with plans to leave early in the morning. There were three more nights after this one, with the band competition starting Friday. That music can run on to midnight and I'm told there are still people playing out in the campground at first light Sunday morning. But I worry if I stay too long the music could turn maudlin and harsh.

The best thing would be to follow one of these musicians home. And get to hear music out on the porch, as darkness starts down by the river and fills the hollow. It could be the same as it was a century ago, the men joking after a Saturday's work, tuning a handmade fiddle or a banjo. "Hillbillies," they were called, because they came from Ireland's Ulster Province and brought songs about "Billy"—William of Orange, whose Protestant army defeated the Catholics at the Battle of the Boyne in 1690.

The newer songs resemble the old. Hear the music in the night air—and the edgy harmonies that could scare you.

> *I wandered again to my home in the mountains*
> *Where in youth's early dawn I was happy and free*
> *I looked for my friends but I never could find them*
> *I found they were all rank strangers to me.*

12

DRAPER DEPOT

37° 00′N
80° 44′W

W hat do you say, old-timer?"

I was shocked. I could hardly manage a nod and a smile as I passed on my bicycle. The man was perhaps thirty years old, in jeans with a plaid flannel shirt. He was overweight and chewing tobacco and didn't look fit enough to actually get on the horse he was leading along the grass by the side of the trail.

I had my bike helmet on, and sunglasses, and I couldn't figure out how he had made such a drastic estimate of age, even if my short beard, worn this summer against the sun, can seem to be more gray than blond. It was the first time anyone had ever called me that and I felt like chasing him down to say, "Look, I just rode this bike all the way from Fries. Let's see you do forty-two miles!" But I settled for walking with a proud ache into the grocery store at Draper for a can of beer and some potato sticks.

Norfolk & Western ran the last train from Fries past

Draper in 1982. The work crews came along and took up the rails and the wooden ties and left a smoothly graded path of cinders and gravel and grass—one train track wide—easing its way along the narrow valley of the New River. It is theoretically downhill, although if you don't watch the river cresting white past the occasional rapids it's difficult to tell this. Let's call it a flat ride through a Virginia state park that is only eighty feet wide. I'm pleased that the trail is here; this stretch of river is rated above my paddling skill level.

It had been cool in the morning at Fries, when I got my bike out of the Jeep. There was a mist lifting off the river, mixing with smoke from a burning pile of trash timber. I installed the bike's front wheel, inflated the tires to forty-five pounds, checked my pack for water and snacks and tools, and made sure I had my red bandanna (since I'd be riding the old train route). Add the helmet and gloves and roll off.

The trail is two cinder paths with dry grass in between, Queen Anne's Lace and clover alongside. The river is off to the right. On the far bank, houses are tucked back against the wooded hillside, leaving room for bottomland corn.

There was a *boinng*ing crunch from the tires on the cinders and stones as I picked up some speed, soon passing the first milepost. It was on trail left; a limestone column with a peaked top, standing about waist high, with the chiseled number: 44.

Another mile out I met a couple of men from Fries who

had just turned to go back. This is their daily exercising and talking time.

"Pretty good deal," one of them said. "We walk out here from town every morning that it's nice. Gets us off the porch and moving a bit."

We talked about the trail and Fries and I asked if they thought my car would be safe parked there in the lot by the N & W caboose.

"We don't have any problems like that here, it'll be fine."

His friend said, "And we've got a new policeman. I hear he's a good one. I think he's out of town today."

I rode on downriver, shifting into the biggest gear so I could get my speed and my heart rate up. I wondered how the state-park people managed to keep motorcycles and ATVs, the all-terrain vehicles, off the trail, especially at night. Perhaps they don't; you'd need a motorcycle to catch a motorcycle. Or you'd set up a roadblock, which would be a tricky affair out here in the woods in the dark.

The creeks come rambling down to the river every few miles, passing under substantial bridges, with stonework below. And now there are signs that warn: PLEASE DISMOUNT AND LEAD HORSE ACROSS TRESTLE.

A hiker heading toward me moved well off the trail when he saw the bike, and whistled his black-and-white springer spaniel to his side. I thanked him as I passed.

The dogs worry me some. I got bitten a few years ago on a bike ride along the Greenbrier River in West Virginia.

A man and his dog stood at the edge of a field, just off the path, watching me approach. I slowed, then stopped and got off, forgetting the standard advice about keeping the bike between you and any animal you don't know. The man and I had a few greeting words about how the day was going, and the river, and the dog, casually but quickly and quietly, reached up and bit my left calf. Blood started seeping from a circle of little puncture wounds.

"She didn't really mean that," the fellow said.

I had a weak, sinking feeling as I biked on into a town. The doctor had the afternoon off. Her nurse said, "Did the dog seem agitated? Was it out of control?"

"No."

"Have you had a tetanus booster?"

"I think so."

She gave me an antiseptic pad to clean the bite area, and a bandage. There wasn't any swelling.

I asked, "So, would *you* take a chance?" We hadn't talked about rabies shots yet.

She smiled. "You're probably lucky."

.　　.　　.

Here on the New River Trail, I'd promised myself, I'd be paying more attention. Plus I'd had a fresh tetanus shot and carried a first-aid kit in my pack.

I was looking forward to Fries Junction, five miles out. It's the place the trains would have approached with caution. The Galax N & W line comes curving in along

Chestnut Creek from the south, crossing the New on a graceful creosoted wooden bridge.

Back in the Ice Jam of 1917, a third of this bridge, including an iron span that rested on the stone piers, was pushed about a hundred feet downstream. That winter the ice had been fifteen inches thick and in the January-thaw breakup the blocks started piling behind a dam just below Fries Junction. The ice chunks rose twenty feet in the air. As late as June of that year, they said, you could still find pieces of ice on the riverbanks.

But Fries Junction is more renowned as a train wreck site. The year was 1928. A passenger train that had left the junction three minutes *early* was backing westward, around a tight curve. A freight train that had left the Fries station twenty-five minutes *late,* and was traveling about fifteen miles an hour, came around the curve from the other direction. The engine of the eastbound smashed into the end coach car of the westbound. Three people were killed and several others scalded by steam.

Some of the train wreck story is told on a marker, next to the picnic shelter and a horse hitching rack. On this day the water below the bridge was calm, pooled by the dam, and two fishermen were out in a boat with a trolling motor.

I rolled on down the trail, the mileposts coming up at a satisfying pace. But I realized that I was paying too much attention to the cinder trail to be able to see much else, and that the bird calls were hidden by the tire noise. I did notice a metallic hum, rising in the air from the hydroelectric plant at Byllesby Dam. A sign on a gate warns people with heart pacemakers to stay out of the buildings.

Fifty yards past the dam and power plant the hum faded out. The river, spilling past the concrete, finds rocks and ledges again. Huge cattails grow in clumps near the water. Blackberry thickets twist up the bank. I rode slower and a butterfly, white with gray spots, flew right with me, staying alongside the hub of the front wheel.

The community of Ivanhoe was ahead, hidden away from the river by the trees and low ridges. I'd driven the winding road into Ivanhoe one day, curious after seeing a documentary that told the story of this "rambunctious little mining town." Lead was mined here during the Revolutionary War. Then zinc, manganese, and iron. They said it took a full acre of hardwood to make enough charcoal to cook off one batch of iron ore.

The train line, when it was built, brought new families to Ivanhoe—at the turn of the twentieth century the merchant class was predominantly black—along with barrels of whiskey and mail-order furniture, and carried the iron and lead ingots and carloads of carbide out to market.

The town was prosperous through the wars but lost its high school in 1953 and then the elementary school, and when the last big plant shut down, the vines started growing over Ivanhoe. New Jersey Zinc abandoned buildings and company-owned houses. One Ivanhoe woman said, "My aunt would just sit on her porch and cry and pray and the honeysuckle closed in on her every day. Every day it grew just a little bit further. There's a couple of things that I hate in this world and one of them's honeysuckle—honeysuckle covers up bad people's mistakes."

Ivanhoe is now just a few buildings downtown and white frame houses with gardens, along the side streets. There's still a proud Fourth of July parade with dogs in the back of pickups. But there's little hope for a new factory. Today's railroad—the interstate highway—runs far over on the other side of the mountains.

· · ·

For lunch I visited J & T Sales, across the road from the bike trail: HIKERS WELCOME: GROCERY, DRINK, HOT DOGS FRESH. On the bulletin board were notices for Australian shepherds and border collies and a "Gospel-aires" concert. A fellow came out and got into a truck that I'd been admiring—a black 1967 Ford F-100 shortbed. He pulled away with the old melodic V-8 Ford rumble of exhaust. If he'd had one of the Australian shepherds, a blue merle, say, in the back of that truck, I'd truly have been jealous.

Men out in the country and in small towns like to ride their dogs in the pickup bed; sometimes the dogs will curl up against the tool box out of the cold wind. Makes you think of a clansman back in Scotland, out wandering the hills with his dog. Once, in Ashe County, in a McDonald's parking lot, I saw a young man with an ax sticking up out of the slot at the tailgate of his truck. Usually you'd put a short length of 2 × 4 in there. In Scotland he would have carried a broadsword.

There were three of us at the trailside picnic table for lunch. A married couple had arrived from the other direction. Her bike was a three-wheeler, and she explained she had a slight inner-ear problem that affected her balance.

Her husband said, "You see a lot of three-wheelers down in Florida. We saw a man in St. Cloud who had one with a motor on it. He had emphysema and he would pedal the bike until he was worn out and start the motor and take it back home. He was on oxygen too, had the tank in the basket in the back."

The woman said, "We go down there a lot. We're Disney fanatics."

They were both wearing gray Mickey Mouse T-shirts.

I asked, "To Disney World? How often do you go?"

"We go three or four times a year and have been for twenty-four years since we took our daughter there when she was two."

"I've never been," I said.

"Oh, heck."

I asked about the trail on ahead and they knew every trestle and curve for the next ten miles.

"We'll ride two thousand miles a year and the majority of it right here on this trail."

They were textile workers and had the same schedule— twelve-hour shifts but only three or four days a week.

The husband said, "To be honest with you, I'm heavy.

But I've dropped thirty pounds and I've kept it off. If it weren't for the bike I'd have a lot more medical problems than I do."

"Ride in the winter?"

"Sure. We'll ride some in the last of January, then February and March. It's better, really, if it's cold so the trail doesn't thaw out and get soft underneath and bog you down."

I finished lunch, drank some Gatorade, took the day's first ibuprofen, said good-bye, and got cranking again. I'm always sleepy after lunch but I was trying to ignore it.

My bike has twenty-four speeds and I was sailing along at the very top of gear range and lung capacity when a startling shout caused me to veer off the trail to the right and two young riders came *blasting* past. My mind supplied thirty seconds of loud hip-hop music (they were wearing headphones) and then a crossfade to bird sounds as the bikers sprinted around the next bend. They were full-on aerobic riders, sensing the trail through blue lenses at twenty-five miles an hour.

A drippy and dank tunnel was waiting. As I entered, my shadow was riding on ahead. At the other end there was a half-circle of rich color: greens and gray and blue. And in the sunlight at the tunnel's exit—an oaty pile of horse manure, delighting several black butterflies.

A long trestle crossed the New River on a slant, carrying the trail to the south bank. The valley began to open and I could see several ranges of hills.

Across the river was the town of Austinville, small and

pleasant. But on this bank the bottomlands lay blackened, with pools of oily water and heaps of slaggy rock.

There was a woman waiting alongside the trail, and she explained the landscape: "Those are tailings from the old lead and zinc mines."

She was a geology teacher from Oklahoma, out with a friend just walking and poking around. They were picking up rocks that showed traces of fossilized algae.

"This was the edge of the ocean, once," she said. "And the lead and zinc in these rock formations just squirted up with the volcanic magma. At mines like this one they just basically roast the rocks again. What you see here now is the junk that's left over."

Austinville is named for Moses Austin, father of Stephen Fuller Austin, who's known as the father of Texas. The elder Austin was in the lead-mine business with Thomas Jackson, who also owned a shot tower, making bullets for muzzle-loading rifles. He built it on a bluff above the river. It stands there today, seventy-five feet above the ground and seventy-five feet *below* the ground. The tower—of limestone block—was finished in 1807 and Thomas Jackson started selling rifle shot by the wagonload. He would carry lead to the top, melt it in a small furnace, tip over the kettle—and the liquid metal would pass through a sieve and round into balls on the way down. The shot would splash into a kettle at the bottom of the shaft. The water was for cushioning, the bullets having already cooled by the end of their long drop.

When you climb the winding stairs inside the shot tower you realize you're looking down into an elegant design—a factory in which the bullets make themselves. It's said the European inventor of the shot tower had seen it all in his sleep. He'd dreamed of molten lead falling as rain.

Jackson's Ferry Bridge is downstream a bit from the shot tower bluff. Mr. Jackson must have been quite the man to see in this area ca. 1800. The hand-drawn ferry that he first operated here was replaced by a bridge in 1938, to carry Route 52.

Then in 1981 the spaceship landed. If you stand by the river and look up 140 feet to the dual span that is the Interstate 77 bridge, you relate it best to the movies. It soars impossibly high and stands red against the overcast sky as in a special effects shot. The bridge crosses the valley at an angle that bears no recognition of the landscape, and gives off a moody, unrelenting roar. The drivers and passengers—crossing—can only have a glance for the river below.

·   ·   ·

I've met a retired truck driver and fly fisherman who once would have tried hard to look over the railing to see how the New was running. In his truck, Lowell Shipe had carried rod and reel and tackle box and vest, and had knowledge of rest stops on the interstates where he could lock the cab and walk down over the hill and get to a trout stream. He had fished the New in Virginia and rivers in the East up to the Battenkill in Vermont.

Mr. Shipe stopped driving a month or so after he recovered from a separated shoulder and some broken ribs from an accident in southern Virginia. He had been reaching down to the floor of his cab for a cassette tape and lost control of his eighteen-wheeler. "It just went sailing." The truck turned over on the interstate and he made an emergency-room promise to himself that he'd leave the road and open a fly-fishing shop. It's on Laurel Branch, which flows into the the North Fork of the New.

On the morning of his accident he was settling in for a day's run to Pennsylvania: the audiotape he was trying to find on the cab's floor was the first part of a six-hour novel, a Christian thriller called *The Oath*. These days for Mr. Shipe it's a pickup drive with a cup of coffee to a tasty spot for smallmouth bass on the North Fork and if the shop's not bringing in all that much money, who cares?

. . .

On the old N & W New River Line the next stop would have been Foster Falls. Once it was a village of a hundred families. The depot's gone, and the hotel and the saw mill; the orphanage still stands, in hopes of renovation. It's a handsome two-story brick building with a wide veranda across the front and sides.

A grassy park runs down to the edge of the river and I took my shoes and socks off and eased my feet into the chilly water. The falls are a series of ledges that extend from one bank of the river to the other. It'd be interesting in a canoe—a two-foot drop, then a foot-and-a-half, then three more smaller ones as the river starts a bend.

.   .   .

I notice the wind is coming upstream, riffling the water so that in places it looks like the current is flowing backwards. The clouds to the northwest have grown higher and darker. I decide I'd better get going. I put on my red nylon jacket. There's a faraway crumple of thunder. A fellow I met on the trail said there's hardly been any rain this year but that last summer, you could usually count on a quick storm about this time of day.

I start riding east. The valley darkens; not enough light for sunglasses. The dark green stalks of equisetum rattle at the side of the trail. The thunder now booms behind me. The wind streams through a willow tree and the thin branches flow sideways.

The rain arrives and the trail turns black with water. There is a dragonfly darting along about two feet from my nose. I ride faster, the tires spinning rain on my bare legs and up my back. A strobe flash of lightning. A sign speeds by on my left: NO TRESPASSING. My bike doesn't hesitate; my mind does. At Fries where I'd started this morning there *had* been a notice tacked to the signboard. The ink was faded. I think it said the trail was closed between mileposts 17 and 19.

I notice some fishing trailers along the river. Then another warning: TRAIL CLOSED TURN BACK. But it's a homemade sign and surely it's out of date because the trail *is* open, although it's much rougher here and the weeds haven't been cut.

I keep riding. I'm getting chilly. The hooded jacket is helping but I should have brought rain pants.

The lightning comes shimmering past in sheets, the flashes illuminating the path. I ride around small boulders and shards of downed trees. I think of the fearful journeys in J.R.R. Tolkien, and the roadside sign in *The Wizard of Oz*: I'D TURN BACK IF I WERE YOU. And I'm also thinking of dogs, and tacks in the trail, or a thin wire stretched across at chest level to tear me off my bike.

Probably, though, in this dark and rain, there won't be anybody around to see me zipping past and soon I'll be back on the legal part of the trail. But that logic dissolves as I slide to a stop in front of an eight-foot-high black wooden gate, chained and padlocked at the center. And in big red letters: NO TRESPASSING.

I realize that if caught, I was going to try to pretend that I thought those signs I maybe *might* have noticed were out of date and that the trail just *used* to be closed, but now I was up against the picture of me trying to climb over that gate and pull my bike up behind me and if somebody'd shot somebody in the butt for doing that and I'd been on the jury I'd have a hard time saying he was wrong.

I am tempted to try it though. I have the feeling that this was the end of the two-mile section that was closed, that freedom is just on the other side of that gate.

My New River Trail map can't help me; it's come apart in damp shreds. I remember a road leading off the trail to the right, a half-mile back. That might mean a long ride in the wrong direction. I balance fear against cold and fatigue—and turn around.

.   .   .

I had to walk the bike up the hill. The rain was slow-falling and dense. The push up to the ridge was a blur; I'd taken off my fogged-up glasses. The narrow paved road led to a highway, which appeared to cross the New River. I'd seen the bridge down below and wondered if I could get back to the trail on the other side.

I noticed a little boy, with an umbrella, coming back to his house from the barn. I rode up to the fence and he came closer.

I said, "Can you help me figure this out about the bike trail? I'm a little bit lost."

He seemed to be about eight years old.

He said, "Did you see all those signs?"

"Yeah, that's why I turned back. Are they serious about not going across that gate?"

"You have to ask Gator King for permission. That's what my daddy does and we go down there all the time. His driveway's back up this road where you came. You can just go up there and talk to him."

"Do the Kings have dogs?" I'd heard barking.

"They do, they have a bunch of them. They raise dogs.

But they just come out and they want to smell your hands and it's all right."

"Can I get back down to the trail on the other side of that bridge?"

"I don't think so; it's a cliff there."

"What if I go this other way? Up the road."

"There's a store up there, is all."

His mom, who'd come out to the porch, called him inside, and I rode on up the highway, away from the river, fighting gravel on the shoulder, and the sudden sideways wind blasts from passing trucks.

Denny's Stop 'N Go was around a long curve. I leaned the bike against a pole and hurried—squishing and dripping—inside for coffee.

The woman at the counter said, "Sorry, I had to pour it out. Just too late in the day."

Outside, three men were sitting on a bench, under the roof overhang.

"How's it going?" one of them asked.

"Cold," I said. "And I got in trouble with the trespassing signs down on the trail there."

"We get a lot of bikes come by here. People get confused about where to go. You could ride over to Allisonia and get back on it there."

"How far is that? Is it hard?" My legs were trembling with the cold.

"Maybe five miles. It's hilly, up and down."

I found a ten-dollar bill, damp, in my pocket.

"Would somebody have time to drive me over there?"

"I'll take you to Allisonia for ten dollars."

His name was Chris. He used some of the money right away to put gas in his Mustang and I put the bike in the back and we were off.

He told me, "Those people who've shut down the trail, they're not all mean. I heard they want fifty-three thousand for the land and they turned down twenty-eight thousand."

Chris said he had one more year of high school, then would join the Marines, hoping to become a state policeman when he got out.

The road dropped down through the fog to the river and the trail and Allisonia. Several small houses and the Trading Post. Chipper Holt and her husband, Don, own the store, rent out canoes and bicycles. And Don offers a shuttle service—he and his truck and his German shepherd, Chelsea, will carry bikers around the closed section of the trail, over the route I'd just negotiated.

"Coffee?" I wondered.

"Why don't I make some," Chipper said. "I didn't put it on before because of the rain."

The New River Trail passes directly in front of the Trading Post. The barrier, I learn, is five miles back up-river. I had been just on the other side of that gate when I retreated.

"We tell people not to try to go over it," Chipper said. "Once there was a woman riding along there with one of those baby trailers and she didn't know what to do so she put her bike and the trailer over the gate and then climbed over with her baby and Mrs. Edwards came out and fussed at them but it was okay and later the woman's husband sent Mrs. Edwards some flowers. She just wants people to pay attention to her."

Don agreed with me that there ought to be better signs. "You get there and it's closed and you don't want to get out on the dangerous highway. Those property owners only get upset if they find out people have rented bikes; it's when they think I'm making some money out of the deal. You could take a church group through there without a problem."

The New River after Allisonia starts being sweet. Claytor Lake is downstream from here a few miles and the calming effect of the big dam reaches this far back. You could rent a house here and fish through the hot days and fool around in a canoe or jonboat, and in the half-light before dawn imagine the early N & W freight trains rolling past.

As I rode east on the old cinder bed the afternoon turned brighter, the storm having moved on. It's an easy pedal out of Allisonia, with the river to my left, on down past the community of Hiwasee, then across the long trestle that bridges the tip of Claytor Lake. The trail from there on to Draper is a bit uphill—good to get the blood moving again. And I wondered, at this moment, which part of your *twenty-year-old* body would you like to have back again. Your legs? Your sense of smell?

There was a cinnamon-woodsy scent coming from a mown field. I passed raspberry bushes and untended apple trees. The sky cleared from hilltop to hilltop. I could see golden and red lights coming up ahead by the side of the trail, lights amid the grass. It was the sun shining through the ears of three cottontail rabbits. They turned to watch me ride up before moving off into the woods.

13

INGLES FERRY

37° 06'N
80° 35'W

Imagine her beating heart, and her glance out the door of the cabin. Mary Draper Ingles is twenty-three years old, the mother of two sons. It is a Sunday morning in July 1755. Her husband is working in a barley field close by. Perhaps there was a moment when the birds stilled, when the dust danced in the sunlight—before the Shawnee attacked.

It is said that Mary Draper Ingles's hair was white, that she was naked, bone-thin, and starving, when she staggered home the following November. She had escaped from a Shawnee village in Ohio.

The Ingles family still owns property on both sides of the New River, at the city limits of Radford, downstream from Claytor Lake Dam. In the mud at the water's edge, river right, are moldering timbers from the old Ingles ferryboat, and there's a rusted cable strand deep in the bark of a sycamore. At one time a toll bridge crossed the river.

They say it was burned during the Civil War by Confederate troops—retreating.

After her escape, Mary Ingles and her husband, William, moved to a safer part of Virginia, but returned to the New River in 1762. The Virginia Assembly approved William Ingles's petition to operate a ferry, at the spot where the Wilderness Road arrives at the New (you can still see a grassy road leading down out of the woods). The Scots-Irish, the Highland Scots, and the German "backsettlers" would pause here on their way down through the long valleys and serried ridges of western Virginia. The Ingles Ferry Tavern provided oats and hay for the animals, brandy and a bed of sorts for the adventurers.

Mary Ingles was eighty-three when she died. Throughout her life after her kidnapping she always insisted on living in a small log cabin without windows. The rock foundation of that cabin remains, outlining the one-room structure near the river. And Bud Jeffries, the property's caretaker, shows me the stones of a cemetery, jumbled up under some white pines.

Bud explains, "What I think happened, when you read history, the people in the wagons when they had somebody sick they'd sometimes leave them at these ferry sites and go on. If they were dead, they'd bury them; if they died later, the people here would bury them."

A marker states: INGLES BURYING GROUND 1782–1861. But no one's been able to locate the true graves of Mary and William Ingles. Bud tells me, "They used the old sandstone tombstones and they crumbled easily and the cattle would get in under the trees. Nobody really put any significance in her grave at the time. It was only in later days when you'd sit down and look at a map and see where she'd been and what the situation was and how she traveled and you'd know how extraordinary it was."

Mr. Jeffries spends most of his time running the outdoor drama performed here four nights a week in the summer months. It's called *The Long Way Home.* Sometimes two hundred people will fill up the chairs to see the Mary Draper Ingles story unfold, with volleys of blank rifle fire and white actors playing Shawnee braves chasing on- and offstage. The young woman in the role of Mary is usually a student at nearby Radford University. It is melodrama with evening crickets and the real New River flowing just beyond its painted image on the stage backdrop, and it can only be an airy tracing of the story.

Among the pioneers who crossed the Blue Ridge Mountains, Mary Draper and William Ingles were the first couple to be married. Their son Thomas was the first baby born on the frontier. The Ingles family was from England, Ireland, Scotland, Pennsylvania. The Drapers were from County Donegal, Ireland, and also lived in Pennsylvania for a time. Both families moved into Virginia, and then in 1748 "came West to grow up with the country." Their settlement—at the present-day site of Blacksburg—was the first on waters running west; a horseshoe bend of the New River was nearby.

That morning in 1755, the Indians killed four of Mary Ingles's neighbors. They beheaded an old man. They smashed an infant's head against a cabin wall. The local militia commander was shot, just after he had killed two Indians with his broadsword.

The warriors burned the buildings, stole horses, food, and tools, and left with five hostages, including Mary and her two young boys. Their route was the Indian war road—the New River. The New north to the Kanawha, the Kanawha to the Ohio, the Ohio west to the Scioto River and the Shawnee's home village. One of the respected accounts of the capture says that Mary Ingles was nine months pregnant, delivered a baby girl on the trail, and later left her behind with the Shawnee.

Both of Mary's sons were taken from her and sent to distant villages. She earned the Indians' trust, by her composure and by sewing shirts for the warriors. She accompanied a salt-making expedition to Big Bone Lick in Kentucky and escaped from there with another white captive, known as the Old Dutch Woman.

They were five hundred miles from home, with one tomahawk and two blankets. They followed the Ohio back east to the Kanawha, with cruel detours up the tributaries until they could find a shallow place to cross. The cold weather came. They dug up roots and ate bark. The Old Dutch Woman went crazy; she tried to kill Mary Ingles and eat her. In late November, after forty-three days of travel, Mary Ingles was found by a neighbor, in his cornfield.

One of Mary's sons died while with the Shawnee, the other returned to Virginia at age seventeen. In the years to follow, William and Mary Ingles had four more children.

A great-grandson, John Hale, wrote this about his family: "Pioneer history does *not* repeat itself."

14

RADFORD UNIVERSITY

37° 08'N
80° 33'W

The young women come running out of the woods and move so lightly they appear to be floating across the grass. Their hair is tied back; they wear close-fitting shorts and loose cotton tops. Most are smiling.

This is an evening workout for the Radford cross-country team. The school has an expansive athletic complex that includes about a mile of practice fields and tracks and trails set along the New River. When I pass through Radford I like to stop here and walk the riverbank.

There is a certain vibrancy in the two universities along the New River—Radford and Appalachian State in Boone. You'll see young people who are proud to be from the mountain communities and farms, who think it's best to be at a small, identifiable school. The same is true for Berea College in eastern Kentucky, on the edge of the Cumberland Plateau. I had hoped to attend Berea, but it's a school for "impoverished mountain youth" and my parents made too much money—my mother worked as a secretary and my father was a mailman. I ended up for a couple of years at Eastern Kentucky State, nearby, but that was a school with big-time pretensions.

And once I was in love with a Berea girl. She was just graduating. Her name was Cuba, and when I would visit we'd sit in rocking chairs on the porch of the Boone Tavern and watch the spring-night rainstorms coming. Cuba was from Alva, Kentucky, deep in Harlan County, where her father mined coal. I didn't get to meet her folks—her world was expanding—and it was several years before I got a chance to travel that far back into Appalachia.

·   ·   ·

At sunset on the New River at Radford the gold light flickers through the trees and gleams off the water. The settlers' accounts, from this region, speak of the "pale green light" in the land they called the Great Forest.

They found hollow sycamore trees big enough to live in. Yellow poplars two hundred feet high. Strong black cherry and hemlock and beech and oak. And chestnut; the Appalachians were a chestnut paradise, before the blight began.

One late-spring morning I walked with a naturalist through an old-growth-forest tract in eastern Kentucky, the Lilley Cornett Woods, one of the last few areas not commercially timbered. There'd been rain, and swirls of vapor followed us up the hillside. Todd Williams, my guide, carried a thin cane stick to hold back the wet branches as we passed, to carefully lift a leaf to show me a pink ladyslipper and a jack-in-the-pulpit, or to warn me away from the furry spines of stinging nettle. As I walked I was seeing the muddy trail and the trees as if in faded black-and-white photographs; he was seeing vivid colors.

"Don't step on the newt," Todd said, picking up a tiny gold creature and putting it onto my hand. "They're running all over in this weather; they're amphibians."

The newt blinked in the center of my palm. It had a slippery, translucent sheen with specks of light brown and khaki.

In the old-growth forest—we were climbing into a stratum of maple, poplar, and basswood—the bird songs drift down from the high canopy of leaves, clear and confident. Warblers and vireos and tanagers: birds that will be in South America come winter.

Todd pointed to the base of a maple with shaggy bark that could be three hundred years old. "See that dark stain all around the bottom of the tree? The yellow-bellied sap suckers drill holes there and the sap leaks out so they can feed on it.

"And have you had sourwood honey?" Todd asked. "It's the best, and the sourwood's the only tree that can grow sideways."

He showed me several thin sourwoods that had changed direction—bending at almost right angles in order to find more sunlight. A big tree falls, blue sky appears, and off goes the sourwood.

A select number of trees had been cut from this forest. The black walnuts were gone, although there was one fine example left behind, close to the ridgetop. "They take it for furniture and veneers. It's the most valuable tree in the woods. This one here is probably worth forty or fifty thousand dollars at retail."

Some trees had been blasted from the hillsides by lightning. Split in two along the grain line or just shattered, with pieces flying fifty yards away. Others simply grow too big for the shallow soil and crash down the slope.

Todd said, "It sounds like half the forest falls when one of these big ones goes down. And if you look you can see where they've been if they've totally decayed. See those undulations—the hollows where the tree was pulled up and then the grassy mound where the root ball was laying? In a way it's like looking at a graveyard. But it's just centuries of energy going back into the soil."

We walked along the narrow trail past white oaks that Todd judged to be six hundred years old. And chestnuts on this ridge, once? Yes, he said, possibly a hundred feet high.

We stopped in front of a chestnut stump about three feet across. The tree probably had been harvested as the blight arrived. There were several healthy-appearing shoots and saplings growing up from the sides of the stump. Todd knows the small trees will die. They may reach ten or fifteen feet but they will die.

"All the chestnuts have been gone since about 1940. There was a fungus in some trees from Asia that arrived at the New York harbor in 1904. You'll find a few chestnuts out West, planted outside their native range, and there's a different strain in Michigan, but aside from that they're gone."

The spores of the *Cryphonectria parasitica* fungus were carried on the wind. The chestnuts in the New York Zoological Park were the first to wither. In the Appalachian forest, one out of every four trees was a chestnut.

Back in the trees we could see a hog pen, built of chestnut rails perhaps fifty years ago, the grayed wood still capable. Chestnut made strong and lovely furniture—"cradles to caskets," they'd say—and shingles and worthwhile firewood. The nuts from the trees fed the hogs and brought in cash money at the markets. White blossoms in springtime brightened the backwoods coves.

In Todd Williams's view we have destroyed our forest and done it quickly.

"There are old-growth trees on this hillside that *saw* all this happen in just the last third of their lives. It's such a short time since the settlers came and now look what we've got."

I asked, "If you'd hunted in these woods two hundred years ago, what would you have seen? Or what would have seen you?"

"Elk. Grizzly bears early on. Black bears for sure. Buffalo. Cougars. Still a few bobcats. Mink, weasel, beaver, muskrat. There were passenger pigeons in flocks of millions and squirrel migrations in the millions too."

Todd had told me that he did a lot of hunting, and I

wanted to ask him about a sensation that I'd felt sometimes, hiking alone in the woods.

"Do you ever feel uneasy?" I asked. "Is there ever a sense
of *presence* for you?"

"Only once," Todd said. "And it was strong. I was pretty
far back in and I got the feeling—I just knew—that somebody was watching me. I was standing there with a six-
teen-gauge shotgun fully loaded and I was very
uncomfortable. Normally a squirrel hunter would think
it's another hunter but I was sure it wasn't. The feeling of
being watched is normally behind you. But this one
wasn't. I was absolutely sure it was right dead in front of
me and I couldn't see anything. I was out on a point.
There was no way to walk toward it. I walked back out
over the ridge the only direction I could go and went
home."

.   .   .

On the way back down the trail we talked about
Kentucky and our own people who settled here. Todd said
that as a child, and even more now, he liked to find the
oldest people in the hills, the ones who knew the trees and
what the plants could be used for. I told him about both
the Wellman and Adams sides of my family, coming to
farm in northeast Kentucky in the 1800s.

Todd asked, looking at me carefully, "Have you heard of
the Melungeons?"

"Yes."

He said, "My family's Melungeon, from down in Virginia originally. Sometimes I don't say that to people right away, even if I suspect they might be Melungeon too."

Todd is tall with dark skin and black hair. His parents, certainly his grandparents, would have said they were "Portyghee"—from Portugal.

When the Scots-Irish came down through the Shenandoah Valley and into the Alleghenies, they often encountered settlements of mountain people—Mediterranean in appearance—who had arrived long before. They were Christian. They had English names. They spoke Elizabethan English and not very well—it was clearly not their native language.

The name *Melungeon* could relate to the French *mélange,* a mixture. Forms of the word show up also in Spanish, Turkish, and Arabic, usually with disparaging connotations. The Melungeon backsettlers said they were Portuguese and that their ancestors had shipwrecked on the Atlantic coast. They were content in their farming communities.

But the newcomers wanted land too and soon there were census takers and lawyers helping out. The Melungeons became Free Persons of Color, then Mulatto, and later, Non-white. Some Melungeon groups accepted the category of Indian, thus retaining at least some legal status.

In both Tennessee and North Carolina, by 1834, Melungeons had lost most of their rights as citizens. In those

states, and Virginia, then Kentucky, the Melungeons gathered farther back and higher in the hills, living close to the
ridgelines in log cabins with windows that were arched at
the top. The children often were ashamed of their darkness, the girls wearing long-sleeved dresses against the sun.

We stopped for a moment at the last bend in the trail.
We could see the parking lot and the headquarters building. There would be others waiting for a guided hike.

Todd said, "It can be a strange sort of discrimination
you feel, growing up Melungeon. Even now I notice it.
People look at you like you're different."

15

PLUM CREEK

37° 08′N
80° 32′w

We've stopped for lunch, the sixteen-foot dark green Dagger canoe pulled up on a sandbar. Shawn Hash, my river guide for the next five days, opens the cooler. We have apples, bananas, and grapes, ham and turkey for sandwiches, sardines, macaroni, orange and tomato juice, breakfast bars—and lots of cheese.

"I *love* cheese," Shawn says, slicing off curls of smoked cheddar. "I go kayaking down in North Carolina and there's a cheese factory outside of Blowing Rock where we always stop and load up."

Shawn is from nearby in Pulaski County and went to school at Virginia Tech at Blacksburg, just over the mountain. He has spent most of every summer of his life on the New River. He and his wife, Molly, own an upscale coffee place in Radford, and Tangent Outfitters. His least happy mornings are spent getting the coffeeshop open when a new employee doesn't show; he's at his best on the water, taking clients downstream for smallmouth-bass fishing, or helping out with a trip like this one into West Virginia.

We'll be traveling about seventy miles and I'm relieved to have Shawn in the back of the boat; this part of the New is mostly wide and flat but does have some tricky Class II rapids and one Class III—Narrows Falls—which I'd seen from the road and decided I didn't want to try alone. The guidebook says: "Be sure to get to shore to scout or carry this rapid. Don't attempt it unless you are very good and have rescue capabilities."

Shawn also worked for several seasons in Fayetteville, West Virginia, for the whitewater outfitters serving the New River Gorge and the Gauley River. He started as a videoboater, in his kayak, chasing along with the raft trips. You ride in the bus to the put-in, tape the clients getting ready. You scoot downriver to the first big rapids and get out on a rock to catch the action when the rafts arrive. Do it again with several more rapids—narrating as you go along—then speed back to the raft company and do some quick editing and duplicating, and when the rafters come back and shower and have a beer they get to see *their* trip on tape. And buy a copy. For the videoboaters the days are fast, exciting, and the season seemingly endless.

Many of the West Virginia river guides spend the winters as ski instructors. That's how Shawn met Molly. They were working at the same resort, far up in the mountains. Molly volunteered to cut his hair one evening. Shawn says about this, "As soon as she touched my head I knew she was the one."

Shawn has a runner's gauntness; he says it's hard to get enough calories in the summertime. He wears a T-shirt and red nylon shorts. His feet are sun-burnished brown, except for the white stripes underneath the straps of his Teva river sandals. I tell him his naked feet—alone on a poster—could be an advertisement. They'd call it a Teva Tan.

I have to wear fleece socks under my sandals, and long pants. I have a black floppy hat with a wide brim. In a canoe the sun hits you several times. You'll feel it directly on your head, and then flashing from different angles off the water. The word *radiation* comes to mind.

Finishing lunch, we sit on a log that's half-covered in sand and watch the river moving toward us.

Shawn says, "When we were kids we used to build an Indian fish trap in a place like this. You'd build up a wall of rocks in the shallow water, and slant it into the bank so it would make a long, narrow V. Then we'd get out in the deeper part and start shuffling down, scaring the fish along in front of us into the V. They'd have nowhere to go; you could just stand on the bank and flip them out."

Earlier in the morning, Shawn and I had done our grocery shopping, then stopped by Java River, where he poured tall cups of coffee for us to take along in the boat.

His outfitting truck is a red Toyota four-wheel-drive with spots of rust that have been fixed and covered with primer, and a green-and-white bumper sticker on the back that says: THE NEW—LIKE IT IS! There are steel canoe racks bolted to the sides and across the top, and bicycle-fork holders inside the bed. This truck could go down the road carrying eight boats and eight bikes.

Shawn slid the canoe off the rack and carried it over-head to the riverbank. "No," he said to my offer of help, "it's easier to do it by myself."

I brought down the cooler and the gear bags and life jackets. He found a place for his fishing rod and reel and settled into the stern seat. I placed one foot in the cool wa-ter, stepped over the gunwale into the center of the boat, then eased onto the front seat.

We started off by going back up the New River instead of down. I wanted a close look at Claytor Lake Dam.

Shawn said, "We won't get *too* close. A lot of turbulence there at the base."

It was a medium flow through the turbines. The New River has been checked, pooled, and portioned out to gen-erate electricity. The release at this moment appeared hesi-tant, the water in a slow cascade down the spillway into a brown and white froth. Then the current gathered itself at the center to head downstream, and Shawn leaned back on his paddle to bring the canoe around, and set us on course for West Virginia.

We passed Ingles Ferry on river right. The town of Radford came up on the same side. A few downtown blocks, then Radford University. The New is wide and almost shallow enough here to wade across, and you'll see students with dogs out fishing and splashing.

We floated under a crumbling old railroad bridge, leaving Radford behind, and drifted around a sharp bend to our sandbar lunch spot at the mouth of Plum Creek.

·   ·   ·

Shawn tells me he believes in the current. It's slow but it's steady and he doesn't see much point in paddling if the river's moving. We'll hit facing winds, he says, and could have some tough work getting downstream. And we're sure to be paddling hard in the few spots of whitewater coming up.

He's interested in what's waiting for me much farther downstream in the big water—the New River Gorge.

"Ever have a throw bag experience, rafting?" Shawn asks, meaning have I ever spilled out of a raft and been pulled back in with a rescue line. "You gotta have a throw bag experience."

He went on, "You never, never know. Things can happen to even the most senior guides. There was a *National Geographic* photographer I took along the river here, Susie. When she went on up to West Virginia they flipped her in Double Z Rapids. Flipped her and all the equipment and everything. Scary."

Shawn also believes in smallmouth bass. And he rigs his rod and spins out a few easy casts. The lure splashes into still water behind a downed tree and he reels it back with flicks of the rod tip.

Ziiiip. Plop . . . Shawn steers the canoe by dragging one foot in the water. I'm almost asleep, warming in the sun, shaded by hat and dark lenses, watching the trees come past on the bank. From downriver we can hear a faint rush of water.

"There's some troll sign over there," Shawn says, nodding to the left bank.

"What do you mean? Did you say troll?"

He laughs. "Trolls. See, there's a forked stick standing up there in the mud? That's where they lean their rods. They make a fire in that ring of rocks. Usually it's Mr. Troll and one or two of his buddies but sometimes Mrs. Troll will be along too."

I keep looking at him.

"And that white plastic garbage bag hanging on the tree limb? That's a sure troll sign."

The water noise downstream is now defined—we're coming to a rapids. I can't see the rocks but I do see spurts of spray in the air, and a *horizon line* on the river; the water beyond is lower. The guidebook calls this a Class II with an "interesting whirlpool on the left."

Shawn is standing in the stern of the canoe, casting back upriver. The current brings us from the right closer to the center. Shawn throws out another cast, reels the lure back in. The canoe is on the quiet, glassy tongue of water leading to the V of the rapids' center drop. The bow passes through the center line of the current and heads left, where the rocks lurk and the whirlpool waits. Shawn sighs, sits, lays his rod across his legs, flips his paddle into the water, and the bow swings straight.

"Okay," he says, as we drive the boat forward to power over the drop. It's a white swoosh and we're through, coasting to river right as Shawn picks up his rod again.

16

PEPPER ROAD

37° 09'N
80° 33'W

We decide to quit the water early today. We're about three miles downstream past the city of Radford, and beyond this point—where Pepper Bridge Road crosses the river—we would soon approach the Radford Army Ammunition Plant. On my map it shows as a vast, vague schematic with blocks of buildings and grids of roads. The New takes a seven-mile loop through the plant's property and you're not allowed to get out of the boat on either bank. We don't want to be in there after dark so we'll sleep back at Shawn's house.

The take-out is river left, under the bridge. We carry the canoe and the bags up to the parking area and wait for Molly to come by with the truck. I'm admiring the bee-balm blossoms flaring red along the water's edge when I notice an awful smell. Shawn does too.

"Trolls," Shawn says. "They live under bridges."

A scuba diver is suiting up, pulling equipment out of the back of a well-kept GMC pickup with a camper shell:

wetsuit, weights, flippers, helmet, and oxygen tanks. His partner is parked alongside and his gear comes out of a small trailer. Shawn's told me about the deep holes in the river, seventy feet or so down in the dark; that's why the scuba guys like this spot.

I walk over to talk with them.

"What do you get to see down there?"

"Rock formations. Colors. There are catfish three or four feet long. We carry lights with us."

"It's important that you don't go alone?" I ask.

"You could get in trouble, get caught in something. There's eddies under the water too, big powerful ones that'll take you downstream fifty feet or so in a hurry."

His friend says, "On a Saturday or Sunday there'll be forty or fifty people in this hole. This is the most interesting thing I ever found and I used to dive on wrecks in the ocean."

I wonder what it's like, being so deep, moving along with the fish.

The other man replies, "I used to fish until I got to swimming with them. Now I no longer have any desire to fish. I see them in their natural habitat and I can just reach out and touch them."

Molly rumbles up in the big red shuttle truck. We tie the canoe on top and make a wide turn out of the parking lot.

Shawn says, "Oh, there it is, there's the smell. Damn."

Molly, driving, catches a whiff. "What is *that?*"

And I can see it in the weeds. A deer's head, rotting, covered with flies.

17

ARSENAL RAPIDS

37° 11'N
80° 33'W

We run Arsenal on the right, zooming down a chute, digging hard with the paddles to miss a boulder. Shawn hadn't seemed concerned and I was trying to forget what I'd read about the "infamous Arsenal Rapids"—that several lives had been lost here. Shawn *had*, though, reminded me to zip up my life jacket for this Class II. I look back upstream and realize that in my solo canoe I might have taken a line to the left and wound up on a rock ledge in a tangle of trees next to the twisted wreck of an aluminum jonboat.

A sudden shriek comes down the valley—two jet fighters on a training run, wingtips almost touching, flying below radar. Higher, we can see the feathery trails of larger planes—at 20,000 feet, the jet exhaust vaporizes white. On the tracks just above the river a Norfolk & Western coal train creaks and clatters past. The waters of the New River are dark green this morning, slowing into a pool after Arsenal Rapids.

"Have you heard," I ask, "about the kayaker who was killed this spring on the Salmon in Idaho?"

Shawn had been telling me about running the creeks in this part of Virginia, sluicing down the tight ravines with the high water, diving the boat over steep waterfalls. If you could find a creek that hadn't been run before, you'd be a "first descenter."

"Yeah," Shawn says, "that was awful. His wife had just had a baby. I'd known about it but didn't say anything to Molly and then that issue of *Paddler* came to the coffee-shop one day when I was out kayaking one of those steep creeks. She was upset when I got home that night."

Our canoe rides steady in the current; you can measure the speed by looking at the trees.

Shawn says, "It's a decision. You don't know. I had a good friend of mine die a year ago up on the Meadow River in West Virginia. I helped teach him how to paddle. I've done the Green Gorge with him; it's where the Green flows out of North Carolina into South Carolina. It's insane. At that time it was probably the hardest thing being run in North America.

"When he died he was paddling great. Some people paddle above their ability and live on luck but he wasn't—the dude was on his game and on the money. But he endered in Coming Home Sweet Jesus Rapids. It was a short boat, and in a steep fall usually you just lean back and put your paddle out behind you in a brace and pop over it and your hair doesn't even get wet. What probably happened was that he flipped backwards and the waves stopped him and he hit his head and knocked himself out and drowned.

"He was a super-awesome guy. He was going to get married soon. He died doing what he wanted to do, you know. Something happened that was out of his control. He's with God now. But you know, I had another kayaking friend who was killed right on the street in Washington, D.C., running after a robber. He was the manager of an outdoor store and the guy got away with the cash and some Patagonia clothes."

Shawn said, "You *can* get too caught up in the high of the thrill; it's like a drug, and athletes always want to be doing something harder. That's when it can get you, but . . . I see these hikers on the Appalachian Trail and they just want to get *done* with it. I passed twenty of them one day and every one of them had their head down and I was like, 'Haven't you guys ever heard life's a journey not a destination?' "

The river makes a sharp swing from north to east. We pass under a railroad trestle; here the track crosses the New and disappears into the side of a limestone cliff. This is Pepper Tunnel; it rejoins the river just on the other side of the mountain. Around the Horseshoe bend as *we're* going it's seven miles by water, through the Arsenal.

A guard tower, equipped with loudspeakers and floodlights, comes up on the right; it's not manned. A sign warns that we're entering the Radford Army Ammunition

Plant and there's to be no trespassing on land or shooting of firearms.

Shawn says we won't be seeing much more than the riverbanks—they're about fifteen feet high and fenced on top. The plant makes rocket fuel, and all the buildings are designed to avoid a chain reaction. In an explosion the roofs blow off as the force travels upwards.

There's a spiral of black vultures over a hillside to the east. And ahead on the river—about forty of the large birds have collected, one is slowing to land, the underside of its wings showing white. The current brings us closer; the vultures pay no attention. They stand in the water and on the rocky beach, and in a line across a log, and all of them seem to be looking in different directions. Up close you notice a cast of the darkest blue in the lustrous black of their feathers.

Shawn and I have been admiring the flight of the bank swallows. They are small brown-backed birds that nest in holes below the edge of the riverbanks. A hundred or so will perch on a wire or line up on a fence. Then they'll rise and pivot and dive in long, swooping arcs to skim the water for insects. Streams of them fly as one—as a swift, fluttering, chittering banner.

The river is narrow through the Arsenal and there's a current pushing the boat but we paddle steadily because it feels like a place we need to get past. And the Radford Plant officials might agree; there's been talk of banning travel on this stretch of the New River.

We approach "the burning ground," on river left. A bench of land above the water and below a hillside. No trees. The ground looks wasted and toxic. BEWARE OF FIRE BLAST AND BURNING RESIDUE. DO NOT LAND ON RIVERBANK. The sign is alongside a set of warning lights and loudspeakers and Shawn says when they're getting ready to set off explosives you'll hear the sirens on the river for miles. Downstream in gravel shallows, Shawn has found residue from this site: white rocket-propellant pellets, unburned. He's used them as campfire starters.

By early afternoon we've paddled the long loop inside the Arsenal, passing the tower that stands watch over the western river entrance. We swing around a turn and the view opens up vertically: low ridges slant down to the river, above them stands Cloyds Mountain on the left, Brush Mountain on the right. These two are green and in clear focus. Far beyond, shading to blue, are the higher ranges of the Alleghenies.

Shawn yells from the back of the canoe, "Usually when we turn this corner we get hit with a ton of wind, right in the face. Looks like we'll be lucky today. Sometimes it's all you can do—paddling just to stand still in the water."

The valley widens out and we begin to see farmhouses, cornfields, cattle. The N & W has tracks on both sides of the river. There are fishing camps—wooden shacks—on the slope of land between the railroad and the water. There's an old blue bus, shot full of holes but you could still camp in it. And on a sandy ledge in one dim copse of birch trees—a mattress on top of a sheet of plywood on top of cinder blocks.

"Troll heaven!" Shawn says. "I wouldn't have believed it. You just lay up there and toss in your line."

Shawn spots a fiberglass skiff tied to a tree.

"I know that boat from upriver. It's got loose a couple of times in floods and it just makes its way downstream. Somebody picks it up and renames it."

The boat is now—in bright blue letters—BR5-49, the name of a retro-country band from Nashville.

We land the canoe at Parrott, and walk up to Sonny's Market for a bag of ice. Parrott is a river community asleep in the sun. A few houses. Sonny's for groceries, mail, videos, and a tanning bed—plus a bulletin-board-ful of trophy fish snapshots.

Sonny's also rents an assortment of camping trailers, in the field leading down to the river. Small and mostly old trailers, some with screened porches. There's a bathhouse for hot showers, and grills for the fish. If I ever wanted to vanish for a couple of weeks I'd come here and hide the Jeep back in the trees.

"I don't know who it was that first came but somebody from eastern Kentucky really liked this place and told everybody there about it," Shawn says. "Most of the people you meet here are from Kentucky."

It is wade fishing that Parrott is known for. Along the western bank the river flows over a series of shelves, with drops of only a few inches. You don't need a boat and when the water's warm you don't need boots. Just stand and spin-cast and let the day flow by, with catfish for supper and a ball game on the radio.

Shawn and I slide the canoe over the low rocks and reach the deeper part of the New before we get in and push off. We've been invited to spend the night at a cabin on the hillside not far downstream. There's a full moon that should lift up over the gap between the mountains; we'll see it from the porch if the sky stays clear.

Hospitality along the river these days can include ribeye steaks, an offer of "local wine and weed," and a soak in a hot tub. We're contributing a six-pack of Old Milwaukee from Sonny's Market. It's a vestige of tradition: I've read that throughout Appalachia, over the years, the one gift that does not insult poverty is whiskey.

18

EGGLESTON CLIFFS

37° 17′N
80° 37′W

The USGS map says, "Creek sinks." Sinking Creek flows strong for a ways through its valley north of Spruce Run Mountain, then it slides underground, becoming marshy and vague as it wanders to the New River. In 1755 the Shawnee Indians brought Mary Draper Ingles and her sons down Sinking Creek, on horseback, riding fast. The volunteer militia that rode in rescue—four days later—followed Sinking Creek, but the trail disappeared in a confusion of ridges and thickets.

I'd been asking about these cliffs, known as the Eggleston Palisades, and as we paddled around a bend on the river Shawn said, "There they are."

The palisades are crumbling browns and grays—Paleozoic Knoxville dolomite—on river right, rising almost straight up and as high as four hundred feet. You could climb them or you could climb into them; they have deep fissures and wooded ravines.

Then we make an even sharper turn, almost ninety

degrees. The unbroken mountain range that is West Virginia has come closer.

The water here is green and flat. The cliffs throw down their image for a quavery reflection. If you wanted to film the Mary Ingles story, this is where you'd bring your cameras for the ending.

Our canoe drifts close under the cliffs. I try to picture the river on an early-winter morning, running dark gray and with a fringe of cracking ice. Four months after she was captured Mary Ingles found her way back into Virginia. Seeing the palisades, knowing that home was close, she made a desperate decision to climb. In his historical novel *Follow the River,* James Alexander Thom imagines that she reached the top by late afternoon, and then could only crawl, "a skeleton covered with bruised and lacerated skin." And that she dreamed of her mother's steamy sassafras tea, with spoonfuls of maple syrup.

Adam Harmon was the farmer who found Mary Ingles. He may indeed have asked, "It's told that this river here goes plumb through the mountains to the O-hee-o?"

And she may have whispered, "Aye. It's where I been."

.   .   .

Shawn and I float through the canyon of the cliffs. The New River in this part of Virginia has a gradient drop of five feet per mile; a slow but insistent current. Ahead of us to the northwest, Peters Mountain crosses the sky. The

West Virginia state line runs along that high ridge, as well as the Appalachian Trail. I have a map that tells me our river will make a turn and go into a gap in Peters Mountain, but for the moment I agree with Mr. Harmon—it just doesn't look possible.

19

PEMBROKE

37° 19'N
80° 38'w

Just under the Pembroke bridge we slide to river right and stop at a concrete ramp running down into the water. It's a privately owned put-in: five dollars to camp overnight, two dollars to leave your car.

"This is Robin and Mark's place. Let's go see if anyone's here."

Robin and her husband have a small house at the top of the property, near the road. The town of Pembroke is a half-mile farther on.

A dog barks as we get close to the house, and then bounds out the door ahead of Robin and her young son, Travis.

"Shawn, look at you, you're so *little*."

Robin is wearing jeans and workboots and a white tank top and she is quite small herself, but she's concerned about Shawn's weight.

He laughs and says, "I'm down to a hundred forty pounds. Just burning up energy this summer, not sleeping much. Molly says I never stop eating."

They talk about the river and mutual friends, the goings-on in Pembroke, plans for the winter season. Robin wants to know why I've got a long-sleeved shirt on in this heat and I explain that I burn easily and tell her a bit about being on the New in North Carolina, and our trip on up into West Virginia.

The dog, a young black-and-tan mix, watches from a few paces away, but seems friendly. Shawn is reminded of Robin's dog Jake, a favorite on the river, a six-year-old German shepherd who died over the winter.

Robin said, "Jake was an unneutered male. The girl dog deferred to him. They had their own rooms, their own couches. Jake got cancer. It lasted about five months. I took him to a lot of vets but I didn't want to take him over to Virginia Tech and put him through all that. He'd go out to use the bathroom in the woods and I heard him yelp with pain. That passed okay but you could tell his insides were disintegrating. One day I decided to take him and have the vet put him to sleep and I carried him to the truck and he stood up a little bit and then he laid down and I think he knew what was going on. They fight it so hard."

She rubbed her arms. "I'm getting goose bumps telling the story." She had a Harley-Davidson tattoo on her shoulder, the colors faded.

I knelt to talk to her son and meet the young dog. "How's this dog doing now, Travis?" I held out the back of my hand but she wouldn't come.

"She's good," he said, "she likes to bring rocks home."

Robin said, "She was scared of the river at first and she'd

see her tail floating behind her and start chasing it. Then she began to swim a bit. Now she picks up rocks from the river—big rocks, sometimes it's almost more than she can carry—and takes them in the house and wants to protect them. She wants me to see them piled up over there. If you pitched a rock over in the field with a bunch of other rocks she'd go get that very same one."

We walked on down to the canoe and said our good-byes, Robin holding Travis's hand, the dog splashing around and biting at rocks.

The George Caleb Bingham oil painting titled *Daniel Boone Escorting Settlers through the Cumberland Gap* shows a trusty light-brown hound alongside Colonel Boone at the head of the procession. And most of the Boone lithographs and drawings include a dog—usually shown looking off into the middle distance, ears alert.

In 1750, Jonathon Plott, when he emigrated from Germany, brought along his favorite hunting dog. He and other settlers also brought wild boars, whose descendants now range freely high in the Great Smoky Mountains. Mr. Plott took up land in western North Carolina and his dog's breedline has stayed mostly pure; Plott hounds are treasured for bear and coon hunting. Also in North Carolina you can buy a local dog called a Mountain Feist, a sturdy little terrier with a touch of beagle—"They're great for squirrels; they can see them high up going from tree to tree." And if you're raising sheep you'll have a border collie or two, a breed from the same region of Scotland as many of its owners' forebears.

One steamy July afternoon in Virginia I went along with a friend as he took his dogs for an after-work swim. He has an old "dog car" that is now only used for their transport. He opens the doors and lifts the back hatch and all five Border collies jump in, each always going to the same spot: two in the far back, two on the backseat, and the shy one on the floor in front.

We drove up a dirt road to a creek's shady spot. My friend and I waded into the chilly water below a small waterfall. We were in up to our waists, our Scots and Irish chests pale in the dappling light. With the grace of water, the dogs had moved to their chosen posts. One watched from the left bank, another was on the right, one standing still on the ledge of the waterfall, another bounding and barking and trying to bite the water as it fell. The fifth dog, the shy and serious one, swam in the water downstream from us, swam from bank to bank, head up and watching for trouble.

20

SAND ISLAND

37° 19'N
80° 40'W

In the time between full darkness and moonrise, I wandered away from the campsite so I could hear the river. There was enough cloudlight already in the sky to sparkle off the wavetops as the current turned past our small island. My flashlight beam hit the water at midstream and bounced at an upward angle to shine on the gray cliffs across the way.

I stood facing upriver; tree frogs singing in my left ear, the water's glassy melody in my right. I could smell the smoke from our fire. Shawn had been collecting driftwood branches all day, tossing them into the canoe.

"Home, sweet home," he'd said, when we passed under an old railroad trestle and saw the island on river left. It was a favorite campsite for him.

He said, "One time I had eleven Boy Scouts on a trip and we tried to get in here before a big rain started but couldn't quite make it. We tied up the boats and I put up one tent quickly and put them in it and then ran around setting up all the other tents. I was hungry and cold and we couldn't find dry wood. I like to bring my own now."

There was a blink of green light at the water's edge, twenty feet away. Then nothing. Then three pulses of green. I walked closer in the dark. Three lights again on the gravel bank. Then perhaps ten more, fading on and off like fat fireflies caught in the mud.

"Glow worms," I said. "Shawn, come look at this."

He walked to where I was pointing with the flashlight. The worms—unlit—were half an inch long, and unremarkable.

"Watch." I switched off the light and we could see an array of luminous pulses. With no discernible pattern. A worm could be dark for thirty seconds and then glow twice.

"Whoa," Shawn said. "That's bright—I've never seen anything like that."

And he said, "Look out in the water there. Lots of stuff going on. Fish are just darting all over. Minnows, big ones—and shiners."

Shawn went to get his rod for a few just-in-case casts out over the excited fish. It was a night feeding; you could see the sudden, angular dance of waterbugs on the surface.

Sand Island was half a football field long, narrow, and close enough to the bank to wade across. Railroad tracks on each side of the river. No roads anywhere near. We camped on a bench of land, well above the water and under the shelter of birches. There was a stone fire ring and someone had built a little table out of scrapwood.

Shawn cooked some freeze-dried fettucine Alfredo and made chamomile tea. We heated water for dishwashing. Watching the woodsmoke curl up into the leaves, we told river stories.

I'd read a book about kayaking the Amazon and now believed that a tiny, spiny fish, the *candiru,* could climb up your urine stream into the urethra and have to be cut out. Shawn's story was better: "When I was working as a raft guide in West Virginia there was a whitewater outfit that had bear wrestling on Saturday nights. A thousand dollars if you could drop the bear: a little guy from Michigan did it. Or the bear would wrestle two women at one time and the big joke was when the handler would yell, 'Go for the berry patch,' and the bear would stick his nose in their crotches and snuffle around."

I slept lightly, listening to the snap of the campfire embers, then the slowing song of the frogs.

Then—a sonorous throbbing noise. An approaching rumbling roar. The slash of a searchlight on the blue nylon wall of the tent. A grinding metallic squeal from the diesel locomotive. Then the familiar thumping clatter of the coal cars as the train curved on around the base of the mountain.

21

NARROWS

37° 20'N
80° 48'W

Tell me of something better than coffee in the morning on the river when the sun's come over the ridge and there's a drift of white fog across the water.

Our canoe is already floating when we wake up. We'd left it solidly perched on a sandbar; Shawn had tied a line from the bow up to a tree on the bank. It would take a lot of water to move the boat, I thought, but the river did rise in the night and the sandbar was gone and the canoe was turned around and twelve feet downriver, bouncing at the end of its line.

Shawn has the number for Claytor Lake Dam on his cell phone's speed dial.

"Yeah," he says, listening to the recorded message. "There was a release last night between six and ten o'clock. It took twelve hours for the extra water to get down here. It's a fast rise when it comes and you can get surprised."

Our gear stowed, we ease out into the center of the

current to float around a bend and see an almost three-quarter moon, still high over Peters Mountain. There's a sharp, thin piping in the air: red-tailed hawks are hunting from an ascending spiral above the river. Apart from the train tracks alongside the water, this seems a private valley of green forest and stone cliffs.

Shawn tells me you can even buy the view.

"What?"

"A viewshed." He points to a mountainside downriver about a mile away.

"Let's say you build a house back here in the field by the tree line. You have a nice view of the water, looking west. And you can see that mountain from your front porch. It's great—nothing but the trees and those pastures, lower down. You want to be sure nothing happens to that part of the mountain so you go find the guy who owns it and you say, 'I'll give you fifty thousand dollars for a viewshed easement. In perpetuity.' He takes the money and signs the paper and he can't change the side of the mountain you're looking at and neither can his heirs."

"Probably nothing would happen there anyway in that time?"

"Maybe. But who knows—it's half a century. Just makes you sleep a little better knowing there's not going to be a big Wal-Mart sign up there or some kind of backwoods amusement park."

The only real profit center I'd seen on this stretch of the New was back at Big Falls, just downstream from Parrott.

A fellow there rents inner tubes and runs a short shuttle service. Students from Virginia Tech and Radford University come out on the hot-weather weekends to drink and yell and spin down across the low ledge drop-offs.

We paddle through a Class II rapids, taking the center line and ride atop a three-foot-high wave train, the curls of water breaking back toward us and spilling into the boat. We'll be wet for the rest of the morning. At the bottom Shawn steers into the right-side eddy. We forgot to bring a bailer so he scoops up the water from the bottom of the canoe with a plastic sandwich bag. It's tedious work and soon I take over and Shawn gets a chance to fish.

He's using a small lure that's black and yellow and white. He throws a long cast into a smooth spot behind a boulder, then spins the lure back toward the canoe. It bobs and jigs, riding just under the surface.

"If you're a smallmouth bass, that torpedo lure looks like a little wounded fish or a little fish feeding on insects on top."

And in a truthful quick splash and flurry of water there's a bass on Shawn's line. He angles the rod tip so the fish comes wriggling to the canoe's side. He leans over and slides his thumb into the pulsating gill, and pulls the fish up so he can ease back the barbed hook.

"See the other holes there? This one's been caught a lot."

The fish has several scars—like pierced-ear marks—along its wide bottom lip.

Shawn lowers the bass over the side with both hands, holding its head into the current so the water can flow through the gills. It spins down and away.

"Do you ever eat them?" I ask.

"No. Some people I know do."

Three more casts bring another smallmouth to the boat. I ask to hold it.

"It's best if you get your hands wet first."

The bass weighs perhaps a pound and a half. It is strong and poised in my hands, as if waiting for a moment of inattention so it could leap back into the river. The belly is white, softly shading upwards to gold, then to the gray and black of the dorsal fin. The scales are black yet hold the sunlight in iridescence. If this fish were to stay out of the water the colors would soon fade.

And I had wanted to see the eye. The pupil is black and, as I've read, is pointed at the end like a seed. James Prosek, the young fly fisherman who published a book of watercolors called *Trout* while he was still a student at Yale, says that the pupil is shaped like a watermelon seed and that in a dead fish the sharp end is pointed toward the sky. It has rotated from pointing straight ahead to vertical. In answering my e-mail query about this detail, Mr. Prosek added, "I have never consciously or carefully watched a fish die. Usually it's either just dead or alive." Our bass is back in the river and gone within two minutes after taking the hook.

It's sardines for our river lunch today. We find quiet water and Shawn opens a can for me and passes it forward on the flat of his paddle. Then crackers, the mustard jar, a slice of cheddar. A bottle of Gatorade from the cooler. The boat stays at the center of the river, moving just enough to make a breeze.

"Tastes a lot better outside, doesn't it?" Shawn says, just as I was thinking the same. We rinse our sardine cans in the river; fish juice in the water.

And there is a chemical tang in the air. "Notice that papery smell?" Shawn says. "It's the only bad smell on the river. It's a Celanese plant, downstream a couple of miles."

"What do they make?"

"Cigarette filters."

We are approaching the town of Pearisburg and U.S. 460, which swings in from the south to cross the New River, then settles in along the bank. Northbound hikers on the Appalachian Trail cross the 460 bridge before their climb to the ridgeline of Peters Mountain. Shawn says the bridge route is unaesthetic and dangerous for AT hikers and that a swinging footbridge has been proposed, about a half-mile upstream, but that local landowners are fighting it.

A coal train comes past, whistling, on river left. Trucks and cars whine along the divided highway on the right. Shawn and I take up the business of paddling. A reach with one hand and a push over the top with the other. The paddle blade leaves the water at the point where it passes the body.

Shawn follows my pace; if I need to rest for a moment or switch sides, he's right with me. We have a facing wind and light waves and the stroke feels like honest work. It's a tug down through the hips and knees against braced feet. I would be happier, though, if we had already made it through Narrows Falls, about five miles ahead. I was thinking about the falls last night. Shawn had mentioned having someone bring us a raft for this day of the trip, but that seemed like too much fuss and so we'll see how it looks for the canoe. Narrows Falls is a "genuine Class III and becomes a Class IV at higher levels."

We paddle around a bend to the left and see the mountains cascading into the river valley. Piney Ridge and Wolf Creek Mountain spill in from the south, then a dramatic drop in elevation and the New flows between East River Mountain and Peters Mountain—at the spot called The Narrows. The *town* of Narrows spreads out on both sides of a horseshoe curve. Shawn points to a white house standing high and improbably alone on Peters; from the front porch you could see most of where we've been today. "That's Jerry and Anna's house; they have a restaurant in Narrows. I hope you get to meet them someday. It's family-style, all you can eat. Great pecan pie."

We pass under a black steel railroad trestle that slants across the river on massive stone pilings, then we paddle on past the town, making the turn back to the north. It becomes clear that Narrows Falls will be waiting where the river divides the two main ridges.

Sometimes when you look at the topographical maps

you can imagine a spy plane's perspective. You are looking straight down on the terrain and you can see the blue of the New winding through the narrow white valleys edged by muted green and brown ridgelines. On the river at The Narrows the cartographer has drawn three rows of chevrons, pointing downstream. And from the high distant view the falls are simply water pouring over the ledges and chunks of gravel. The photographer Arnout Hyde, Jr., has a morning-lit color picture of The Narrows, taken from a plane at about seven-hundred-feet altitude. Wispy white fog covers the valleys; dark green ridges come into the center of the photograph and then disappear. The ocean of fog rolls on toward the higher mountains far back on the horizon.

From river right we hear a gentle, atonal music. Another dozen paddle strokes and I realize we're hearing the half-frightened calls of cattle from their pens at the Narrows stockyard.

The sound follows us around a bend and fades into the rippling-liquid warnings of Narrows Falls. We take the canoe to river left and get out, clamber up the bank, and follow a dirt road to a place where we can get a good look.

Shawn says, "You always have to check this one out first. Some people do choose to carry around it. You haul your boat up to the road here and walk it on downriver. Takes a long time with all your gear and stuff. Not much fun. And a lot of people will just decide to go for it and flip it in there and swim."

The falls are roaring; it seems like a lot of water to me.

It's a three-foot staircase, with a final drop that looks to be about ten feet and lots of boulders in between.

Shawn looks across the river, "What you want to do is come in on the right side there along the first shelf and we'll make a kick left—you basically *boom* right back this way, almost sideways to the river, and then we'll turn into the current and run dead center."

There is a fisherman on the rocks down by the pool below the falls. Shawn has noticed he's caught a bass that he shouldn't be keeping.

"That fish there's in the slot," he tells me quietly.

And he climbs on down the bank a few yards. "Hey, having any luck?" He has to shout over the noise of the water.

The fisherman says, "Not bad, I guess." And he lifts a stringer out of a bucket. They're all about the same size. And the wrong size. If you want to fish for bass in this part of the New River and stay legal, you'll carry a stick with a mark at eleven inches and another at fourteen. You hold the stick up to the fish and if it fits into the "slot," you have to throw it back. This size bass is in its most productive breeding years.

Shawn yells, "Looks like those are in the slot."

The man grins, shakes his head no, and turns away.

We leave and walk back along the road. Shawn pulls out his phone and calls information for the Giles County Sheriff's Department.

"I'm going to see if they'll get a deputy down here on this guy."

But the connection's weak and he can't get the number

and punches the phone off in frustration. "Hell with it. Maybe somebody else'll turn him in."

We get the canoe ready for Narrows Falls, tying the dry-bags in and securing the cooler with a heavy black bungee cord. I snug up the retainer on my sunglasses, after a minute's thought about taking them off for the run. My life jacket needs to be cinched, as well as the straps on my river sandals—I've heard a strong current can pull them off your feet.

If my heart is pounding it's lost in the roar of the rapids. We swing out quickly, to line up on the right side of the approach, and rest there with paddles poised—"Wait till I tell you"—as the boat hesitates before the first plunge.

"Go!" Shawn yells, and we're down the ledge and the bow is swinging and I'm looking directly at the riverbank as we dig in to surf across the top of the waves pouring under us. I bang my paddle hand hard on the gunwale. I can feel a sideways slip. The boat rocks.

"Paddle! We've got it!" Shawn sounds like it's fun. And suddenly he's pulled us into a sweeping turn and we're bouncing off rocks and smashing through waves but we're in control and moving straight and then powerfully over and through the last drop.

The boat spins off to an eddy. We're about half full of water.

Shawn's grinning big. "Good work. That's about as much action as you'd want in an open boat. We'd've been swamped if we got the least bit sideways on a rock up there."

My smile is one of assurance, and I sit up strong in the

boat, having suddenly become an expert whitewater paddler.

"Shawn, you know if you'd reached the sheriff on the phone and he'd sent somebody down to check that guy's fish, we would have for sure spilled right there in front of both of them. Or else the man would've had a gun and everybody'd have been in trouble."

Shawn says, "That's exactly what I was thinking, too. That's just the way things work."

We bail out—Shawn's found a Clorox bottle and cut the bottom away to make a scoop—and paddle on in a pleasant trance. The river's wide and breezy.

Two Vs of Canada geese move downriver with us, honking and circling to land for a minute's feeding in the shallows, then spooking and rising to search again. I can see perhaps thirty hawks curling on the thermals over the valley.

Then, rising steam from a smokestack and a grid of sparkling lights—the Glen Lyn coal-fired power plant stands on river left. U.S. 460 crosses back over the New River here, running on west. There's a town park with a red N & W caboose. A camping trailer flies a NASCAR banner above a Confederate flag. The picnic shelter is happily occupied by the Meadows family birthday party.

I sit on the gravel bank under the bridge and wait for Shawn to come back from the store with ice and a couple of pieces of fried chicken. The water's clear and a bit warm here just below the outflow pipe from the plant. There are thousands of tiny black snails on the underwater rocks.

Not far away, upstream along Rich Creek, in 1928, a young man—the oldest of sixteen consecutive born sons—found a shiny glassy stone while he was throwing horseshoes with his father. He eventually realized it was a gift from a long-ago glacier. It weighed 34.46 carats. William Jones sent his diamond to the Smithsonian Institution, just a year before he died fighting in Germany at the Battle of the Bulge.

22

SHUMATE FALLS

37° 23'N
80° 51'W

We are deep in West Virginia on a Sunday morning. The air is chilly, colder than the river. If you had a cabin on the west ridge above us you'd be in sunlight but down here on the river the warmth is two hours away.

I sit in the canoe sideways with my feet in the water as we float through the rising mist and Shawn throws out some casts and tells me about a blind fisherman he knows. Why not, the guy's good, Shawn says; in many ways he's better.

That fisherman might have missed the black mink slyly peering out of its hole on the mudbank, and the heron that we startled off a sandbar, dangling a snake it had been trying to swallow, but the owl's *hoohoo*ing, and the wind-shifting sound of the falls would've painted night pictures for his campfire.

And then sometimes a rifle shot, echoing from back over the ridge. No houses are around; we've entered the

Bluestone Recreational Area. There's a dam and a good-sized lake not far downstream. On both sides of the river the hunting and fishing access is made easier by Jeep trails, red lines on the map. You take to the woods these days on a Honda or Kawasaki ATV four-wheeler; you pack the camping stuff in and tie a deer on the front going out. Shawn says he's seen one guy bring in a generator for his TV set.

I'd been a little concerned about our campsite the night before. It was between a trail and the river. But Shawn had walked up to scout it and called back, "It feels good. And look, somebody's almost built a little house."

There was a firepit and a clothesline, a level tent space, and a low enclosure made from carried river stone. A good-time camp for sure but it was empty when we decided, near dark, to come off the river.

We built a fire for comfort and cooked dehydrated red beans and rice on the butane stove. Some green grapes from the cooler. Fig Newtons. And cold beer with ibuprofen; it had been almost a twenty-mile day and I wanted some ease for sleeping.

Shumate Falls had been nasty. We'd heard it from a couple of bends back upstream. Shawn picked a river left approach for the first rapids, then we both got out and walked the boat through scant inches of water, across a ledge back to midstream. A century ago the river was the only way through this part of the country. Flat-bottomed wooden bateaux were used, carrying goods upstream as well as down. Dynamite made it possible. You can still see man-made channels, with straight edges, through many of the rapids. Here at Shumate the blasting left a knife-edged rock right at the bottom of the main falls. You line up for the entry, pick up speed tipping over the shelf, and roar down five feet of whitewater as the knife rock waits to grab and gash your boat. Shawn had his paddle hard in the water as we veered by.

We talked that night about the men who had done the dynamiting and the ones who tried to make a go of wresting those heavy boats *upstream,* with poles and ropes, carrying loads of salt and tobacco and farm produce. In a few generations their sons became coal miners and railroaders. And they still farmed, wanting to live where the view from the porch was of meadows and hillsides. Stubborn, quiet men, who held families close.

Shawn said, "When I first came up to West Virginia to work at the ski resort I think I was a little bit apprehensive. You hear stories, you know. And one night I had left work real late and was trying to drive all the way down home for my days off and was pulling a trailer back—I'd brought my snowmobile to the mountain. About one o'clock in the morning the hitch broke loose and I slid around a curve and the trailer and the back of the Toyota wound up in the ditch.

"It was dark. I was broke and tired. And a man in a truck stopped behind me. He had a battery lantern with a good beam. He didn't talk much but he said the hitch should be welded. He chained up the trailer to the back of his truck and I followed him to his house, where he let me sleep on the couch and in the morning while I was eating the breakfast his wife fixed he was out in the driveway with his welding rig. There was nothing for me to do but say thanks and leave, and over the years I've made it a point to stop and see them and we talk now about all kinds of stuff."

.   .   .

We float into midday, the sunlight now reflecting in yellow pools on the river. A final Class II rapids and a hard paddle to river right where Shawn's wife, Molly, waves from the high bank—this is Indian Creek and the trip is over.

Molly is frustrated; she's been dealing with phone calls for Tangent, and customers at the coffeeshop. Shawn and I are moving more deliberately, still at the river's pace.

The gear gets stowed on the truck; the canoe on the top rack. And we drive up out of the valley on what West Virginians call a lane-and-a-half road. The pavement's a little wider than one car needs and the sandy shoulders are even and broad. The idea is that you drive down the middle and when you meet another car both of you drop one wheel off the road. If somebody doesn't pull off? They're from out of state.

23

RAINELLE

37° 58'N
80° 46'W

An herb wizard named Tim sits in a broken-in recliner with a crocheted comforter across the back and his white poodle-mix dog named Jane tucked in between the chair's arm and his legs. His life's collection of postcards—filed in plastic slips and arranged by country of origin—are in cartons along the wall. On the shelves there's an array of antique metal banks and scrimshaw and the complete works of Oscar Wilde.

Tim Thomas's bachelor apartment is in one of the white wooden buildings that comprise his Appalachian Root & Herb Company. It's close by the Meadow River, a few blocks from a church with a splendid, glowing, chestnut-wood sanctuary, in a onetime logging town called Rainelle.

It's said as "Ray Nell," and, with the accent equal on both syllables, almost begins a melody. Whenever I notice Rainelle on the map I think of wet mornings and brooks that spill off the ledges into the rivers. And of damp earth and misty-green ferns. Millions of years ago the wet compressed ferns became peat; as the mountains heaved up, the peat became coal. The United States has long been burning the ancient green plants of Appalachia to make electricity.

I took a helicopter ride once with the director of West Virginia's Environmental Protection Department. We flew low over some of the mountaintop removal strip mines; they were far more horrendous from the air than could be imagined from the ground—the sites usually aren't visible from the major highways. The director had some reclamation projects he was proud to show me; contoured hillsides that had been hydroseeded with grass, and successful swatches of small trees. But yes, he admitted, that ruined strip site down below, leaching iron oxide? It was indeed one of the state's many orphaned mines. And the one below the next ridge as well.

At the airport I thanked him for the tour and asked an oh, by the way, question. What would have happened if coal had never been discovered in the state? He paused. My meaning was clear: the real money from the minerals had been made by out-of-state business people and West Virginia was finding it tough to even clean up the mess. I had a tape recorder running so I was surprised by his answer: "I've thought many times about what West Virginia would be like if Mother Nature or God had not put coal in these mountains, and I frankly have had to conclude that perhaps the state would have been better off without the coal."

In Rainelle, Tim Thomas asked me if I'd seen the cut-down mountains, stripped to shale and mud, with oily green and rusty runoff.

He also wanted to know if I'd brought a coonskin, in case I planned to take pictures.

He said, "ABC and NBC, they've done documentaries about West Virginia. It's about as far from the truth as you can ever get. The first thing they do is they find an old shack and they tack up a coonskin on the side of it. As old as I am I've never seen a window covered with a coonskin or found anybody that ever has. And they go way back up one of these hollers and find a poor ignorant woman up there and ask her a lot of stupid questions."

.　.　.

The early generations of settlers had a golden century. It is about a hundred years between the violence of the frontier and the coming of the coal trains. The settlers who came across the Allegheny Mountains, who came down the Greenbrier River and the New, the ones who crossed the Cumberland Gap and went up the Big Sandy Valley in Kentucky, lived in self-subsistence and peace. They grew their food, they hunted, they made most of what they needed, and for cash money for the rest they'd brew up whiskey to sell, or float a raft of logs down the river to a mill town. Coal was like a creature that jumped up out of the ground and grabbed them by the throat. The men took the jobs, they left their homes for town, becoming proud and prosperous, but then, in many cases, broken and depend-ent. Or they gave up trying to live on land ruined by mining, land for which their great-grandfathers had sold the mineral rights.

Across the street from our house in Ashland, Kentucky, stood an outsized stone building known as the Mayo Mansion. We shopped downtown in the Mayo Arcade. We understood, growing up, that the Mayo family had a great deal of money. We knew them to be helpful in the community—Mrs. John Mayo was my Cub Scout den mother. But there was also a sadness that was somehow connected with the name. I learned later that a Mayo ancestor had been the leading speculator in eastern Kentucky mineral rights. John Caldwell Calhoun Mayo traveled through the mountains making deals for as little as fifty cents an acre. Mayo's wife would often go along on the buying trips, by horseback into the hills. She wore a skirt that had tiny pockets sewn inside—the pockets held twenty-dollar gold pieces. The landowners signed what became known as the "Mayo Deed," five typewritten pages that gave a company the right to take away the underlying minerals and to tear up the land in doing so. No one, though, could have pictured today's huge strip-mining equipment, and many of the mountain people didn't believe railroads would ever be built; they thought their coal and oil would stay undisturbed.

.   .   .

At the Appalachian Root & Herb Company, you will find drying bundles of the newly popular St.-John's-wort. It's a shrub that grows with bright yellow flowers and is used medicinally to treat depression.

Tim said, "These old strip mine sites are full of St.-John's-wort. You can get all you want. It grows in waste places, alongside the roads. We couldn't sell it for a nickel and then it was on television about depression and now everybody and his dog wants St.-John's-wort. I'd seen it sold in Germany, and it must be good because it's prescribed there. They put all their roots and herbs through the same process that we do here with the FDA for prescription drugs. So you know what you're getting. This country's different; we used to sell directly to health food stores. You could sell them poison hemlock, they wouldn't know the difference. Or care. The health food people are a bunch of cracked-up nuts. I have no confidence in the herb business as far as doing anybody any good."

"Really?" I ask. "You mean as far as health is concerned?"

Tim said, "You know you hear about all these big stories, people say how the Appalachian people used to use roots and herbs? Well, they never heard of them."

"People around here?"

"You can't find anybody in the whole state of West Virginia that ever used any kind of a thing that came out of the woods except goldenseal."

"Goldenseal for what?"

"For sore throat, mouth sores, they do know that. There's a lot of goldenseal. We get right now about thirty-five dollars a pound for it. But when it's processed and sold, I figured out you can go to the Rite Aid store and it comes to thirteen hundred dollars a pound, when they put it in the capsules."

I'd seen black cohosh in the woods. The plant has a tall white cylindrical flower, with tiny petals. Some people call it black snakeroot, or bugbane, because of its pungent odor. And I'd noticed posters in stores, offering to buy black cohosh, "wet or dry."

Tim says, "Yeah, that's a big thing now. They use cohosh for female problems. It all goes up and down. One time here we were buying mayapple by the ton. The drug companies were after it. We sold a lot that year, thirty thousand dollars' worth."

I wondered how much someone could make in the woods, cutting St.-John's-wort and cohosh, perhaps coming upon some ginseng.

"Well ginseng, we're paying three hundred dollars a pound, but that varies. I just run into this guy the other day down in Russellville. He's been bringing bags full of stuff here for twenty-five years, he and his wife. Goldenseal, he's brought mostly. And black cohosh and blue cohosh. He told me, 'You know in the last twenty-five years every dime me and my family's had we got from you. We put all the kids through high school and one of them through college. But hell, you got to work.' "

Tim lifted his dog, Jane, off the chair and took me on a walk around his business. In the sunny side yard there were wooden racks draped with shaggy sheets of bright green moss.

"This is a great part of our sale, for the florists. The moss stays green for a long time. We sell berries and bark, lots of dried wildflowers.

"Let's go in the office a minute," Tim said. "I want you to take some ginseng home."

I'd never seen the root, only the plant in the woods. He brought out a large plastic bag full of ginger-colored twisty roots, some thin and viny and some thick and stubby.

"We went to Hong Kong and watched them sell ginseng the way they sell expensive watches; they lay it out on green felt.

"In China they believe that the shape is critical, that a ginseng root shaped like a hand, for example, can be beneficial if you have a hand problem. They'd really like this one; here, why don't you take it with you? See how it resembles a man; there's the head and arms and legs?"

"How much ginseng does somebody bring you at a time?"

"Oh, somebody who really paid a lot of attention could maybe get five pounds in a year. But people don't dig ginseng for money. It's like playing golf; it's a challenge to find it. See, the younger people, they don't have no interest in it at all. The older people still like to dig it. My brother, he'll go out, stay all day, walk all day, might not find but three or four stalks but he's happy. Ginseng's a mystery in the woods; it'll hide from you. And it gives you a thrill when you find it."

24

BECKLEY MINE

37° 47'N
81° 11'W

Recipe for a Depression Flower
Arrange coal in a bowl or flat dish.
Mix 6 tablespoons water, 6 tablespoons salt,
6 tablespoons bluing, 1 tablespoon ammonia,
and stir until salt dissolves. Pour over coal.
Use Mercurochrome or food coloring for different
hues. Add more of the liquid along to keep
it growing.

There is a coal flower in a glass case in the small museum at the Beckley Exhibition Coal Mine. This flower has been growing since 1919; it is frothy with white and green and red crystals and is now three times bigger than when it was started. An older woman standing next to me said, "I remember when we had those in school. Those would be the only pretty things you'd see of a winter."

Another older voice, a man who had served in the

mines, was telling friends about the ponies. "Looks like there would be a picture of a pony."

"What did they do?"

"They hauled cars. One of them saved my life one time. The ceiling was falling up ahead and the pony turned around and started running. I jumped on his back and we headed out of there. I was lost; we were about a mile back in. But the ponies know where they are."

The exhibition mine, they like to joke now, is a gold mine for the city of Beckley, which is about twenty miles to the west of the New River. People come by busloads, buy their tickets, and ride in a small battery-powered railcar, called a man-trip, through a low opening in a hillside and into a mine that was once owned by the New River Coal Company.

Our guide is a veteran miner, retired and energetic. There were lights along the tunnel walls. He stopped the car about a half-mile in.

"We'll just wait here to see if anybody's getting claustrophobic. If you are I'll ride you back out and refund your money. From here on you're stuck."

Everybody laughed. It would be all right as long as the lights stayed on and the miner was right there on the car with us.

But the lights did go off—with a snap. And there was a gasp at the darkness.

Our guide said, "Just thought I'd give you a feel for what it was like when it's really black. All the men had for light in the early years was these open-flame carbide head-lamps."

And we could hear him assembling his own light.

"You drop a little water in here onto the carbide, stir it around a little. It starts to make acetylene gas and there's a striker flint on top."

A hiss in the dark, and *whoomph*! A bright stream of blue flame jumped from the lamp on the guide's forehead. We could see ourselves again, but the light barely reached the wall of the tunnel.

"They used mules and donkeys and Shetland ponies in here to haul the cars out. The animals stayed under-ground; they'd only go outside two or three times a day, with the coal. After about three months in the pitch black the animals *do* go permanently blind."

The guide switched the string of electric lights back on and started up the man-trip. We lurched and creaked along the tracks under the dripping black roof and around a long curve. His narration picked up in volume:

"The temperature's always fifty-six degrees in here. These tunnels run for three miles back under this hill. And there's plenty of coal left. This is smokeless bituminous coal, low sulfur. The seam is between thirty and thirty-six inches high."

I've talked with retired miners in several parts of Appalachia. They will say they never wanted their sons to go underground, but often that happened anyway and the men were usually proud. They would tell me about accidents in the mines: one said, about a fire back in the mountain, "They hauled me out and another guy for dead." But the coal miners say there was something private and quiet about working down in the tunnels, away from daylight and cars and telephones. You worked for yourself, mostly, with no one standing over you. You went in without a fuss and left with a day's work, or a night's work, done.

Our car stopped in front of an open coal face, cut about twelve feet back into the vein. There was a pick and shovel and an auger leaned against the wall, and a tin lunch bucket.

"That was their food and water for the day; sometimes it was sixteen hours. You'll see that bucket has three sections to it? The bottom part is for drinking water. Your wife'd put sandwiches in the center there. And the top would be for dessert, if you were lucky. They called it a 'fried surprise.'

"The miners would be by themselves in these holes. They could hear somebody maybe a quarter mile away, but the company felt like if they were two together they'd be talking instead of working. So it was up to you how much coal you could get. You'd drill your dynamite holes, three of them, with that breast auger there. Twist up pages from the Sears & Roebuck catalog and fill them with black powder and push it all back in the holes and stick in your fuses and light it and run back down the tunnel and hold your ears."

I carry on my key chain a round brass tag stamped with the number 81, which I bought as a souvenir. It's authentic and worn thin, from a West Virginia coal mine and an unknown miner. He would have carried a string of these "81" tags into the mountain each day; after the dust would settle from the blast he'd be down on his knees to shovel out the coal, loading it into a two-ton car waiting on the track. A pony would pull it or he'd push it out. The weighman, at the scales outside, would pull off the numbered brass tag so the miner could be paid. In *this* mine, in 1919, our guide said, that was twenty cents for a ton of coal.

There was also a wooden canary cage on the muddy floor of the workspace.

"There's natural gas in these mines. Same kind of gas you have in your homes but there they add something to it so you can smell it. In here you can't tell it. But the birds have lungs like we do, only tiny. So you'd carry that canary in and keep listening for it all day."

25

BLUESTONE DAM

37° 38'N
80° 53'W

Let's just say that the Dairy Queen in Hinton, West Virginia, is the center of the universe. Have a chili cheese dog and a Pepsi and listen to stories about coal mining and railroads and rivers. Hinton is where the Greenbrier River arrives from the east to meet up with the New, coming from the south. And the CSX rail line, which has been following the Greenbrier Valley, turns north at Hinton. You can see all this from the glassed-in back porch of the Dairy Queen; it's built out over the river.

The tracks were laid in the 1870s by the C & O, to connect the waters of the Chesapeake Bay with the Ohio River. The line from Virginia was built through farm country and over a few mountains, with the real construction challenge beginning downstream from Hinton where the New enters a deepening gorge.

The C & O made coal mining a practical proposition, and more than a hundred mines were running by the

1920s, with towns to house and supply the miners. Trains still roll through but the coal industry has shut down—the lower section of the gorge is deserted. The main businesses now are whitewater and tourism, with the United States Park Service watching over the New River Gorge National River and the nearby Gauley River National Recreation Area. If you're a kayaker in New Zealand, you'll know about both rivers. They are famous for dependable whitewater rafting, and the Gauley, with a hundred rapids in twenty-five narrow, twisting miles, has legendary status.

About fifteen outfitters run trips down the New and the Gauley. Many of the companies insist their guides learn the history of the region, have an appreciation for what's been here before. One outfitter makes sure its new guides walk or bike the length of the lower New before getting out on the water.

It also helps to talk with the old-timers. A retired C & O engineer named Carl Vest sat in a chair on the empty second floor of a railroad museum in Hinton and told me this story. It's about Thurmond, downriver. Thurmond was a railroad boom town that is now almost ghostly (it was used by director John Sayles as the setting for *Matewan*). With enjoyment, Mr. Vest related the following event:

"This fella died there and they's having a wake at his house and when everybody'd left except two brothers and they were there with the corpse, one of them said to the other one, 'I believe I'll go up town and get me some beer.' The other one said, 'No, you stay with him and I'll go.' So they couldn't agree on that so they said we'll just get him out of his casket and put his arms up around their necks and led him along there and got him up and went to the beer joint and when they got there they set him down on the bar stool. Leaned him up against the wall. They said he was the best-dressed man there. They started drinking a little bit and a big fight started and somebody went over and hit that dead man. Knocked him off the stool. So one of the boys said, 'You've killed my uncle!' And the man said, 'Yeah, but he drawed a knife on me.' "

. . .

Later I stopped by a clock museum in downtown Hinton to talk with the Reverend Charles Wood. He'd just returned to the area, brought his collection up from Florida. He and his wife, Mona Kay, were both born here, about twenty miles south in communities along the New River. Much of the land Reverend Wood remembers as a child is now under Bluestone Lake.

He said, "I left home early because I played in a string band—old-time music you'd call it. We played on WJLS in Beckley and traveled a lot. But I was around home to help when all my family had to move because of the dam. They got a fair price from the government, I think. Nobody wanted to go but back then people were hardy, they could accept change. Some of the cemeteries were moved but usually then you couldn't find the coffins because they'd been in the ground so long. When people moved out they'd come along and tear down the houses. There were two big brick homes up from the river a bit that they blew up with dynamite."

Charles Wood's home was in the area known as Crumps Bottom, close to Indian Creek where Shawn Hash and I had ended our canoe trip.

"What did your family do?" I asked.

"My father owned the ferry at Bull Falls. It was a big ferry barge, held three automobiles, and for some reason I can't remember, the gunwales were made out of pepperwood. I was helping to run that ferry when I was twelve; you'd use a long pole and push against your shoulder, walking from one end of the boat to the other. My dad also farmed and he had a truck that he'd haul with, a 1928 green Chevrolet."

"Do you know where they came from, to begin with, your people?"

"I know my great-grandfather came from Ireland. Michael Quinn was his name, and he was married three times. He was a boatman too. He'd run those bateaux upriver, carrying produce. Crumps Bottom was deep, loamy soil, the best land I ever saw. There were rows of corn there a mile long. And they'd sell tomatoes, corn, beans, cabbage—all the way to Bluefield and Princeton."

.   .   .

You can drive to the top of Bluestone Dam. Go through Hinton and cross the river, then turn left when you see the

Dairy Queen and take highway 20 south for a mile. You can park and walk out and see the blue-green lake on one side and the diminished, flood-controlled New River on the other. There's a riverside park where the construction camp used to be.

Bluestone Dam has a 1940s look, with vast swoops and steps of concrete crossing the valley. Lichens grow on the surface now. The engineers at Bluestone say the structure will last another fifty years. People who don't approve of dams take comfort in the geologic fact that over the span of a million years, water against rock, water wins.

26

MEADOW CREEK

37° 48'N
80° 55'W

If you want the good photograph of Joy Marr, the one where she can't keep from smiling, bring her to the riverside.

Place her deep within the creased stronghold of Green Sulphur Mountain, Irish Mountain, Plumley Mountain, Hump Mountain, Smith Mountain, and Backus Mountain—the ridges drained by Farleys Creek and Sewell Branch. And Lick Creek and Laurel Creek and Panther Branch and Meadow Creek, the larger stream, itself fed by Lefthand Fork, and by Beelick Branch, which runs off Beelick Knob, at 3,225 feet, passing forgotten strip mines on the way down.

There's a community where Meadow Creek ends at the New. Twenty or so houses and fishing trailers, a grocery store and a post office on the road leading down to a parking area by the boat ramp. Put Joy Marr right there, sitting on an ice chest, the canoe's bow already in the water, and take the picture on the first morning of a three-day trip.

Joy and I are discussing provisions: a dozen eggs, bacon, potatoes, chicken *cordon bleu*—lots of salad greens and fresh broccoli. And we're looking at the map. We're doing the Upper New, from Meadow Creek down to Stonecliff. It's the easiest part of the New River Gorge, with a few Class III rapids, "heavy water" but not overly technical.

One way to scout part of this route is to drive out to the Grandview overlook—several miles downstream from here and fourteen hundred feet above the river. The Park Service has an office there, with a visitors' center and a natural-history display. And a photograph of Joy Marr: *First Woman to Row the Upper Gauley: 1978.*

There's no need for Joy to talk much about this, or that she's guided more than a thousand raft trips on the New and the Gauley. Today we have low-adventure intentions, more interested in birds and cloud formations.

Joy laughs. "I don't even like to paddle that much. This is the daydreaming part of the river. We'll use the paddles when we have to make a move but I like the regular speed of the water just fine."

We shove off with a canoe full of tents and sleeping bags and water jugs and extra clothes. In a small drybag clipped to a thwart with a carabiner I've got sunscreen, two energy bars, a thermometer—I like to check the water and air temperatures—and a folding knife. Joy's river knife is clipped to her orange life jacket, and we both have emergency whistles. She's wearing red shorts and has her sandy hair pushed through the back of a blue baseball cap.

The boat rides at balance. Joy steers from the stern. I'm

the crew. It's assumed she can request a draw stroke (I'd reach out with the paddle blade and pull in toward the boat), or a pry (a push away, with the bow moving sharply in the other direction). It's also assumed I'll spot the dark, hidden rocks before we slam into them head-on.

We wander the river in silence. It seems like Joy is humming a song but she's not. She'll stand for a moment in the back of the canoe, then we'll slant left to follow her line through the rocks and bouncing waves.

Our direction is almost due west, through Rocky Rapids, then Grassy Shoals Rapids, and long, slow miles in between. Then, high on the left, we see the cliffs at Grandview. The New is about to take a swoop to the northeast, then back to the southwest, followed by tight turns to the north, east and north again—it's as if the river were a chain that you'd drop in loops on the ground.

· · ·

In Charles Frazier's novel *Cold Mountain,* a young woman, Ruby, is surprised to learn that not everyone can call the names of the trees on the surrounding hillsides. It was something she grew up with, knowing. She tries to teach these things to Ada, the older, well-bred woman who's taken her in during the Civil War. One crisp, dry autumn day Ruby and Ada sit in the hayloft, looking out at the woods and the fields in their North Carolina cove:

—You say you want to get to know the running of this land, Ruby said.

—Yes, Ada said.

Ruby rose and knelt behind Ada and cupped her hands over Ada's eyes.

—Listen, Ruby said. Her hands were warm and rough over Ada's face. . . .

—What do you hear? Ruby said.

Ada heard the sound of wind in the trees, the dry rattle of their late leaves. She said as much.

—Trees, Ruby said contemptuously, as if she had expected just such a foolish answer. Just general trees is all? You've got a long way to go.

She removed her hands and took her seat again and said nothing more on the topic, leaving Ada to conclude that what she meant was that this is a particular world. Until Ada could listen and at the bare minimum tell the sound of poplar from oak at this time of year when it is easiest to do, she had not even started to know the place.

. . .

In this steep valley of the New River, if you would come to know the trees, it might be in their descending order. At the breezy canyon rim: American holly, mountain laurel, scarlet oak and scrub pine, hickory. On the slopes halfway down: poplar, white oak and red maple, sassafras and dogwood and beech. The sycamore, birch, and willow are the river trees. And the paw-paw, with its bananalike fruit. And you'll find the Kentucky coffee tree—the settlers would brew up the seeds if that's all they had.

The royal paulownia tree is a new arrival that has sprinkled itself on winged seeds throughout the gorge. It has huge, drapy leaves, and, in the spring, pale violet blossoms. You'll hear it called the "princess tree," being named after Anna Pavlovna, an ancestor of Queen Juliana of the Netherlands.

The paulownia came to the New River with the railroads; a shipment of dishes would arrive safely cushioned by paulownia seed pods. And these days a descendant of the coal-town family who bought the dishes might go into the woods at night to saw down a thirty-foot paulownia tree. The wood is soft and light and valued in Japan, especially for sandals. It's illegal to cut trees within the National River boundaries, but the Park Service has caught and convicted only a few of the paulownia poachers.

In the evening, when we've set up camp on an island on river right, upstream from Quinnimont, Joy collects some sprays of jewelweed—we've been talking about how effective it is against poison ivy.

Joy says, "I rarely catch it. I wash in the river first of all and crush the leaves and the stems and rub them up and down my legs. Some people keep jars of jewelweed crumpled and let it get all nasty and oily and greasy, just in case they're fishing or hunting and walk through poison ivy."

Joy spreads a branch of jewelweed out on a pool of clear water.

"And here's what amazes kids."

Wet, the leaves take on a silvery iridescence.

"Little kids love to see that shimmer, and once they

learn about it they love to show someone else. This time of year, too, on river trips, we like to find the staghorn sumac. You know they have those red seed pods? You can squish it up and make pink lemonade. It's a real nice surprise."

.   .   .

I sleep on the island inside the reverberance of steel. The coal trains roll through the gorge, through the night. There is the silence of the river and the crickets and the wind, then the metallic pulse of a diesel horn at the whistlepost. As they pass, the rail cars bang against one another—clashing in shock waves up and down the river. At bedtime I had seen flashlight beams moving along the water at Quinnimont. Men looking for something, frogs perhaps. They were about a half-mile away. Their lights are in my dreams too.

In the morning we go looking for the monument that honors Joseph Beury. The first carload of coal from the New River Gorge was shipped out of Quinnimont. That was in September 1873. The C & O Railroad was brand-new and Mr. Buery, late of Pennsylvania, now the owner of the Fire Creek seam, was the victorious operator. We walk up the hill above Quinnimont's small switching yard, crossing the tracks and the road. Joy recognizes an empty building that was once the post office, and in the weedy trees out back we find the stone obelisk, inscribed JOSEPH L. BEURY. It was dedicated around 1920, in the boom time for the New River coalfields. There's a black iron fence, collapsing, around the monument's base.

· · ·

We begin our second day on the river with the long loop of the New known as Stretcher Neck. The C & O carved a tunnel through the mountain and saved five miles of track building, so the river runs alone around this tight corner of the gorge. We start with the Quinnimont Rapids—a Class III, then McCreery, White House, and Dowdy Creek Rapids—all IIs. They are miles apart and we float in between, listening to birds calling through the trees. And we hear a cluckle from the riverbank: three wild turkeys poking about in a clearing.

"That's rare. They don't let you see them," Joy says after we've eased past.

I've been told by hunters who go in with bow and arrow and full camouflage to wait out a long day for a shot that the turkeys are very smart. The hunters wear masks. "A wild turkey can see you blink."

We pull over at a campsite worth stopping early for. It's a sandy bottomland with a fine-gravel beach, with no trails leading in; anybody else who'd show up would likely come by boat.

I dry my feet and put on sneakers and go for a stretching walk along the moss-covered rocks, through the birch trees, back to where the land turns sharply upwards. Garden Ground Mountain will stand above us in the night.

After supper Joy tells me about Joseph Beury. It's pronounced "Berry." She knows the *town* of Beury from her raft trips in the Lower Gorge. From Quinnimont, Mr. Beury moved downriver to open a new coalfield and build his future on the steep slopes of what became known as Beury Mountain. In old pictures his town looks like it could have lasted. Two-story homes, a large white Catholic church, a company store, built of stone. Colonel Beury's own home had twenty-three rooms, a swimming pool, and stables.

Joy says, "It isn't even a ghost town now. We'd stop there several times a year on the raft trips and climb up over the tracks. You used to be able to see some of the foundations but that stone's all crumbling away now and the vines just grow over everything."

No one lives in the Lower Gorge anymore. Joy knew the last one, a woman whose Haitian grandmother had worked in the Beury home. For many years Melcina Fields was all by herself in a hollow on Beury Mountain.

"The raft guides and the train people knew Melcina. She wouldn't talk to you much but she would take help. Somebody put up sort of like a lawnmower shed for her to live in. And we'd bring her food and Pall Mall cigarettes. The train guys would leave her off some coal; she had a little stove that she cooked on. She liked Dial soap and she'd nail the wrappers and Doritos bags up on strings in the trees. It was sort of like folk art."

I sleep in long underwear, and tie the tent flap open so I can listen to the river. In the morning we have coffee and pack up fast and start out paddling instead of drifting; the water's wide and slow after we clear some wake-up rapids below our campsite.

Joy has plans to drive to Virginia in the evening. She and a partner, a former Navy Seal, are setting up an eco-challenge race for next spring and they want to scout some locations. The canoe part will be on the New River, starting at Claytor Lake Dam.

She tells me, "I met this guy two years ago when the Navy sent some Seal teams down to train on the Lower New. The company I worked for, Class VI, would take them out at two in the morning and they'd use night-vision goggles and run the rapids. I was one of the guides who went along to help, but they sure knew what they were doing. So now he's ready to retire from the Navy and we're thinking about setting up this eco-adventure business."

The water is still enough that the birds seem loud. Turkey buzzards sweep and caw overhead and we hear the dry rattling of a pileated woodpecker back in the trees. Soon we head to river right and the landing at another of the used-to-be coal towns.

The sign on the tree has served well through the years: DENT'S CAMPGROUND THAYER WEST VIRGINIA: PUT IN TAKE OUT SMALL BOATS

It's wide flatwater here, and you could easily use a boat with a motor to fish a mile or so back upstream. You'd be careful though about your drinking, because the Class III Silo Rapids waits below.

There's still a small community and a church along the tracks at Thayer. And Mr. Dent's campground at the river's edge.

Joy says, as we get closer, "There's a fire going but I don't see anybody around."

We pull the canoe halfway out of the water and walk up the boat ramp. There's a grassy field with about twenty camping trailers. And a large steel-roofed shelter full of river treasures. A copper moonshine still. A carbide lamp. Grandfather clocks. A front wheel from a 1927 Chevrolet, with iron hub and wooden spokes. An oxen yoke. Hundreds of Mason jars. A farmhouse kitchen bell, and West Virginia license plates going back so far that the first one doesn't have a year. A photograph of a twelve-year-old Thayer coal miner. And lots of fishing photos—grinning young men holding mud cats that come up to their chins.

There's a campfire ring on the bank, with log ends smoldering. We probably missed some good stories last night. The smoke drifts out over the water, staying with us as we start downriver in the canoe, and I realize that I know it's oak that's burning. I think I could tell applewood by the smoke as well. It's a start.

27

FAYETTE AIRPORT

38° 01′N
81° 06′W

The Fayette County Courthouse, sandstone and redbrick, sits handsomely on its own block in the center of town, framed by white oak trees and an expanse of grass. Local teenagers and a dog or two like to sprawl out on the lawn. Town authorities recently decided the kids were a disgrace, close to being loiterers, and banished them from the courthouse grounds. A retired teacher, Eddie Bennett, an emphatic Republican, who has a storefront office on Main Street—G. EDWARD BENNETT: OPINIONS EXPRESSED—offered a compromise. He went to the hardware store and bought two park benches, which he donated to the town on the condition that the kids could use them. He asked two of them to put the benches together and loaned them the tools. Now you can usually see teenagers around again, vaguely near their green benches. The oldest Fayette County residents might find this fuss amusing; there were public hangings—for murder and rape—on this courthouse lawn, within memory.

Fayetteville's young people can have a slight hippie look, and it blends well with the techno-rad style of the kayakers and rock climbers and mountain bikers who roll into town on the weekends, car and truck roofs festooned with gear.

The most money you can put into a parking meter on courthouse square is a dime. Walk a block or two and you'll find a whitewater store, a bike place, the Hard Rock climbing center, Blue Ridge Outdoors. And there's an art gallery run by two former river guides who also operate a birdwatching tour business: WE BIRD HARD!

Within half a block: the state's best pancakes at Cathedral Cafe, pizza at Bazil's, or chicken fajitas at Sedona Grill, plus the old Fayette Theatre, now featuring a local musical production of *Sleeping Beauty*, with a West Virginia state trooper as the prince. These are two-story buildings around the courthouse, with rentable offices on the second floors. A lot of people who come to Fayetteville spend time trying to figure out how to stay.

There's a phone booth at one corner of the square. I've been to the airport before and seen the sign: RIDES $5. I've seen the plane in the air, crossing high above town and looping out over the gorge. I've heard stories about Five Dollar Frank and figure I'd better call home just to sort of announce the fact that maybe I'd fly with him tomorrow? There's tension at the other end of the line. I promise to phone right after we land in the morning, but then drive straight out West Maple to see if Frank can go up right away.

Mr. Thomas started his airport in 1946, using the seventy-eight cents an hour he'd been making in a steel mill. It was fresh air and flying he was after. The Army Air Corps wouldn't take him during the war because of a hearing disability. He has a hangar that can shelter a few planes, a flat-roofed office he built with river stones, a paved runway that's adequate for his Cessna 172s.

There's a sign by the fence: BACK IN FIFTEEN MINUTES. WILL FLY. FRANK. But I see him coming across the field from his house. He's tall, bent, and has a few broken bones in his walk. He has thick-lensed glasses, a sturdy hearing aid.

"Are you by yourself?" Frank asks. "There's a two-person minimum. Five dollars each. It takes two for me to break even."

"Just me."

"It's been slow today. We'll wait and see if somebody else shows up."

He looks back to the west. "There's gray clouds coming up I think we can beat."

"What if I paid the ten dollars myself? Could we go now?"

"If you want."

And I follow him through the gate out to his plane.

"Can I sit in front with you?"

"Absolutely. Let's do it."

Frank shows me where to step on the wheel strut, and how to buckle the shoulder harness and pull the seat forward some. He turns some switches and the engine catches, the propeller flutters to a full spin.

I talk louder. "How many people today?"

"I've been up maybe six times. But it gets busier in the evening. A bus could roll in here with maybe thirty people on it."

We taxi slowly along the runway, heading for the top of the strip, slightly uphill. A turn to kick the tail around. A pause while Frank powers up the engine against the hold of brakes, then a roaring takeoff roll, using all the runway that Frank's paved. And because the strip is on a ridge it seems like the land falls away more than the plane leaves it.

In a book that Mr. Thomas wrote about his airport he tells the story of a pilot who landed here one day, wanting to sell a new-model plane. Frank had heard this aircraft wasn't good for short fields. The salesman wanted Frank to take a ride to prove otherwise. Frank said no, let's first see you go out of here with just yourself. And, he writes, the pilot agreed:

> . . . but apparently he did not judge the heat, the rough field, and the altitude, which all add to a slow takeoff. On his run he used all the field and went out of sight. He had found the little hidden ravine that slowly leads to New River Canyon. After two and one-half minutes we saw him climb out of New River Canyon, safely homeward bound never to return to Fayette Airport.

．　．　．

Frank and I head east, past Fayetteville, to approach the gorge and the highway bridge that crosses it. The engine settles into a flackety drone. The plane buffets lightly in the clear air.

I have been warned but am not prepared for the sight of the New River Gorge from an airplane. We drift out over the edge, beyond the meadows and the bordering sandstone cliffs—and the earth suddenly *drops*. There's a gasp and a shard of panic deep in my body.

We turn upriver. Frank points down. "Lots of boats every evening."

And I can see the tiny flotillas: reds, blues, yellows—the whitewater rafts coming down through the gorge to the final set of rapids. We can see buses—painted the same colors—lined up at the take-out.

"Kaymoor," Frank says, nodding at the west wall of the gorge. Some of the Kaymoor coal mine infrastructure has been saved; there's a trail leading from the rim to the mine site, halfway down, and wooden steps going to the old townsite at the river. The tipple building remains, and sheds and the ruins of coke ovens down along the railroad tracks. The workers and their families lived either at Kaymoor Bottom, or high above, at Kaymoor Top, and rode tramcars down and back up. There's not much left now and the trees and the weather threaten the rest. Kaymoor is more archaeological site than ghost town.

Frank says, "It looked a lot different back in the fifties,

even. Now it's getting so you can't tell anybody was mining here."

We make a tight turn out of the gorge, then another, to line up with the home strip. We fly parallel to a four-lane highway. "That's the thing about Frank," someone had told me. "He wouldn't be afraid to land on an interstate even if he had to. Some of these younger guys don't know how to get out of trouble."

I'd been asking people if they'd fly with Frank.

"You bet," people would say. "One time he hit two horses in a pasture but he's never lost a passenger."

The Cessna loses speed and altitude. I see Frank's airport up ahead, the narrow grassy clearing centered by the strip of pavement. As we are about to float down, still fifty feet high, the wings are rocked by a crossing blast of wind. My hands fly up, my boots push against the floorboards. Frank, paying no attention really, flicks the steering yoke, adds power, and lays two wheels on the runway, then settles the nose. I've heard that sometimes he lands with one wheel *off* the runway, on the grass, simply to save wear on his brakes.

I realize that Frank Thomas is a damn fine pilot, especially for this circuit, which he has flown uncounted times. And I tell him so.

"Aw, I doubt that. I've been flying forever—fifty-six years. I'll be seventy-six my next birthday and I'm still legal. They just delivered me a new engine for one of my airplanes. Rebuilt, same as new. They did it down in North

Carolina. Cost me a bundle, a little more than nine thousand dollars. I'll have to fly some to get that paid for."

In his book, *It Is This Way with Men Who Fly,* Frank Thomas writes about a friend's death, in 1973:

> A gloom of sadness has reached Fayette Airport. Pete Puckett, the flyer among flyers, is dead. All agreed among men that there has been none with such a love for flying. Where else would it have been fitting for Pete's passing than under the wing of an airplane. After a full day of flying, he landed, stepped from his plane, and went to sleep.

28

THURMOND

37° 57'N
81° 04'W

At four A.M. I'm obsessed about my car keys. I'm in a big antique bed in the front room on the second floor of the County Seat B & B in Fayetteville and I couldn't say for sure that I haven't been awake since about two. It's the morning of my whitewater raft trip and I can't figure out what to do about the keys. I'll lock the Jeep, that's just sensible. Change into my river clothes, but I don't have a belt loop on my shorts to clip the key ring onto. Do the life jackets have pockets? Maybe I could leave the key under a tire but everyone knows that trick and why am I so worried about it anyway out here in the center of West Virginia?

The birds start at five and I'm finally getting sleepy at six but the alarm rings at six-thirty and I'm showered and dressed and downstairs right at seven.

"Going on the river?" Pat Bennett smiles, pouring coffee. "Looks like a great day. I think the water's up a bit."

Pat is Eddie Bennett's wife. They run the B & B together, bought it when they retired; she was a teacher as
well. Mr. Bennett's little office downtown is just a place
she sends him in the middle of the day.

"It's my first time," I tell her. Two guys sitting at the end
of the table just nod and keep on eating pancakes. They
look like kayakers. Also at breakfast, a man and his wife
who were startled late last night when a huge determined
dog clambered up the stairs after them, dragging its chain
and tie-out stake. The dog belongs to the Bennetts' visiting
son, and wanted to sleep inside.

I drive out to Class VI River Runners, crossing the New
River Gorge Bridge, turning north along a lane-and-a-half
road, driving through a wet-gray fog with bright lights and
wipers on.

I walk into the main building and find Scott Hill behind a counter and a sign that says 9:00 LOWER NEW.
Scott's the trip leader. Two boats are going; I'm on his raft.

"First time?" he says.

"Yeah."

And I ask about the temperature. It seems chilly to me
but Scott's wearing shorts, with a fleece pullover. I'm wondering if I should rent a wetsuit.

He says, "You know, I don't like to make a recommen-
dation on that because if I say no, people will complain if
they get cold. You just have to decide for yourself. This is a
right-on-the-edge day. It's sixty-two this morning and the
water's chilly but it could turn hot."

I decide to get a suit—it's $13.50—to protect against scrapes as much as the cold. And I notice a plastic bucket on the counter, also labeled: 9:00 LOWER NEW.

"Car keys?"

Scott says, "Just toss them in and they'll be here when you come back. No trading up, though."

"You been using that line all summer?"

"I use it every year all summer."

I've never put on a wetsuit before and halfway into it promise that I won't ever do it again. But if I have to I'll buy one of my own. The fit is tight, the black neoprene sweaty and creepy against your skin, especially if you start thinking about who's worn the suit before—even if it's carefully washed at day's end.

I put on fleece socks and my river sandals, find a helmet and a paddle. Picking up a cup of coffee, I stand on the porch watching the buses pull up and people running back and forth to their cars, forgetting things, going to the bathroom absolutely one last time, talking fast, the adrenaline starting to stir.

Brant Scott says hello. He's the guide for the other raft. He's bigger than Scott Hill, and smiles more easily.

The trips are leaving every fifteen minutes, going off to the Lower New and the Upper and Lower Gauley. Some of the blue and white buses have had the back cut off at the level of the seats—they're huge pickup trucks—to carry the large deflated rafts, as well as the rafters. Our group is riding in a shorter bus with the rafts strapped on a trailer behind.

Everyone's talking as we pull out of Class VI, but at the high bridge there's a hush. The fog is vanishing in spots and you can see stretches of the river below. You can even spot the froth of the rapids.

We roll past Fayetteville, past the town of Oak Hill, and turn off the main highway at Glen Jean, then wind down the narrow road following Dunloup Creek as it falls into the gorge.

Brant gets out to help unload and inflate the rafts, and Scott takes up a position at the front of the bus. He's in charge of both boats. He faces us with a stern look.

"Everybody got a helmet? They're all one size, you adjust them with that strap in the back, like a baseball cap. The rule is: helmets on at all times in whitewater. When we get on flat water and we're floating and it's hot, we can take them off for a while.

"Life jackets?"

The blue vests had been waiting on the bus seats when we got on. They're professional grade, with a wide flap above the shoulders, designed to hold your head up out of the water.

"We're going to put these on and cinch them down real tight. If you slip out of that jacket you're history. If you're out of the boat we're going to pull you back in by the straps—not your arms. It's easy to dislocate someone's shoulder if their arm is extended above their head."

Scott looks carefully from face to face.

"Any medical conditions I should know about? If you

might have an asthma attack? If you've had a heart bypass? Allergic to bee stings? Don't surprise me on the river. Talk to me privately after we get off the bus if you want to."

He speaks more quietly. "If you're having doubts about this trip now's the time to decide. You may be here because of peer pressure, and you really don't have to go. You can ride the bus back up to Class VI and go for a walk in the woods while you're waiting; nobody's going to think anything about it."

He holds up a paddle: white plastic blade, aluminum shaft, T-grip handle. "This is the most dangerous thing you'll see today. In the boat, make sure you keep the palm of your hand over this grip. When we get into big water things start flying around and if you've got this T-grip exposed you can break someone's nose. It's happened. To me."

We all try out the proper hand position, now more afraid of hitting Scott than of falling out.

"Remember," he says, "the fun is in the boat; the fun's not in the water. If you do swim, the first rule is *hang on to your paddle.* Then get your head up and your feet downstream and *find me.* Look at the raft, look at me, and I'll tell you which way I want you to move."

He holds up an orange nylon bag with a rope looping out of the bottom.

"This is a throw bag. I throw it; you grab it and hang on with the rope over your shoulder and we'll pull you in. I'm very good at throwing this bag. Look to me as soon as you get in the water 'cause chances are I'll hit you right between the eyes with it."

Then Scott releases the tension. "Let's get started. The water's high today; we should be scooting right along. The morning part's easy, the big water doesn't come until the afternoon. And by the way, lunch is a time, not a place."

We climb out and stretch and then help carry the rafts down a concrete ramp to the river's edge. Scott divides the paddlers into two crews. I'll be in his boat, along with two women, a young married couple, an older man. We choose our seats. The women want to be up front; they seem to have some experience. I walk to the number-two spot on the right.

"Here's how you stay in the boat." Scott takes a paddle and steps into the raft.

"You've got three anchor points. Slide one foot up under the tube in front of you. Sit right out here on the rim of the raft. See how this strip is black and the rest of the boat's white? We like to say 'one bun on black.' If you try to hide down inside the boat you can't reach the water with your paddle, and that's your third anchor. That paddle in the water keeps you stable."

The guides check the fit of our life jackets, trying to yank them off over our heads. We walk the boat into the water and climb in. Scott's in the back, centered. He has dark hair in a ponytail. He's barechested under his green life vest. Several carabiners are clipped to a rope that's tied around his waist.

Both boat crews go through paddling drills in the shallow water. "Easy forward." "Forward," which means faster. "Back left," meaning the right side paddles forward and the left side paddles backward. "Back right" is the reverse, with the right side paddling backward and the left side forward.

I'm not paying much attention, looking instead out at the center of the river where the water roughs into whitecaps. Soon, we're paddling that way, angling to meet the main current. Scott says, "This is the Thurmond riffle. You might put your helmets on in case something's up."

We cross the last flat water and suddenly the river rises big in front of us. The bow dives down and we're slammed by waves—I'm almost knocked off balance and back into the boat. We're through it quickly and glide under the old railroad bridge that crosses into the junction at Thurmond.

Scott says, "That was a pretty big hit there."

And the woman across from me has the same look in her eyes as I must have in mine. If that was a *riffle,* then what happens in the Class Vs coming up downstream?

We had a glimpse of the restored Thurmond Depot, and you could see a few of the old three-story brick buildings and a rusting water tower, but the river demands your focus, as we sweep past the town into a bend heading east. We're lucky to see even this much of Thurmond. The alternative put-in is five miles downstream from here at Cunard, where on a summer Saturday morning there can be a hundred rafts lined up for their runs. At lower water levels that's a good trip, down to the take-outs near the high bridge. But today the New is running fast at five feet above normal and starting at Cunard would mean we'd be through the Lower Gorge and finished before lunch.

We come to a stretch of calm water, and there's time to talk. Our bow paddlers are Sara, who's an obstetrician, and her friend Carrie, a nurse—they're from Pennsylvania. The young couple, Craig and Ellen, work in a hospital emergency room in Charleston, the state capital, forty miles away. He's a resident, she's a nurse. Craig's father, Carter, is the other paddler on my side. He's a retired doctor, and now, he says, mostly a rock climber.

Of the group, Carter seems the most comfortable. He's been down the river a couple of times before, with his son. Craig is worried about Ellen, who didn't really want to come and seems chilly and underdressed, wearing shorts.

My confidence level goes up a bit, learning that I'm in a boat with three doctors and two nurses. I'd heard stories about the early days of rafting on the Lower New. The guides didn't carry radios and when someone would be badly injured they'd hike up to the railroad tracks and break into a call box to phone for help.

Scott tells us that he's had EMS training and this year went through eighty hours of wilderness first-response school. He also says he's had doctors on trips who were panicky and next to useless in an emergency. The Class VI trip leaders all carry radios—Scott says a helicopter can get someone to the hospital in Charleston in sixteen minutes.

I suppose Craig or Ellen could wind up in the emergency room from which they'd taken a day off.

We pass the site of Buery, on river right. Scott points it out. It's a trick to imagine the buildings, the houses, the coal tipple. You can see some straight-line indentations, at various angles along the mountainside, and hints of wrecked steel and masonry.

A roaring sound starts to build. Scott puts on his helmet. So do we. He stands for a moment, before steering the raft slightly to his left. Our rudder is Scott's paddle.

He says, "This is Surprise coming up; it's our first big one, but it's a straight shot. If you swim you'll spill out into the pool at the bottom and we'll pick you up. No big deal."

I'd read about Surprise in my guidebook: "From the top it looks like an ordinary riffle, but halfway through, paddlers realize they are in a funnel and all of the water is converging toward a mountainous double wave."

I tighten the chest and waist straps on my vest, and still try to breathe deeply. My right foot is jammed hard under the seat tube in front of me; my left foot is braced against the tube behind me. I make myself slide farther out on the black edge of the raft.

The noise stops. The birds seem to hesitate. Our paddles wait in the air. We watch the line of bubbles in their soft dance downstream.

Five feet from the edge—now I can see all of Surprise Rapids below—Scott says, convincingly, "Forward."

The boat is powered down through the wave train. We

start bouncing; my paddle blade misses the water, thrusting against nothing. Carrie, at the bow, is tossed back onto my legs.

The front of the boat dives to accept the force of the second wave and the water slams into my chest. I spill into the center of the boat, then scramble to regain the edge. We rock sideways and punch through another wave, skidding past boulders, and slide into the pool at the bottom of Surprise.

No one speaks. Everyone grins. Our raft is heading directly toward a rock wall, but Scott simply drops his paddle to his right and we come about in a circle.

We hold in the eddy to watch Brant's boat tilt over the top and smash down through the two big waves. There's yelling from his crew—I don't think we yelled. They raise their paddles together in a river salute—I don't think we'd do that.

Brant's boat leads us downstream, slowly again. Scott, knowing, after Surprise, that he has our attention, offers more coaching.

"In these rapids to come there'll be times when you think you should paddle but you really shouldn't. You'll think you *need* all of a sudden to steer the boat, that you're seeing something I'm not. Don't do it. Watch this next Class II."

We're picking up speed, not paddling. Scott yells, "See that big rock ahead right in the middle? Most of it's submerged? I'm going to miss that rock by about six inches. You have to let me do it."

And we're going faster, still with paddles held high, straight at an ugly boat-rending boulder. It *does* seem that the women in front will have to save us, because surely Scott's misjudged this time. But they wait. And inches from collision the bow kicks right and we swoop down over a ledge and then—"Forward"—instantly turn back to the left to miss an even nastier array of rocks. Then we're out. If Scott had taken a wider line we couldn't have made the critical move.

"Every trip is different," Scott says. "I know that rock and I know where it will be at different water levels so I can trust it, but there's something new happening every time down the river."

We zip through a playful wave-train rapids, riding the roller-coaster center, with the front of the raft lifting at sharp angles. I realize that from the shore, you don't have the right perspective on the rapids. You can't see the holes in the water, the places where the boat sinks down before a rising wave. From the riverbank or especially the road, a true ten-foot wave might appear to be half that high and harmless.

"That's Jump Rock ahead," Scott says. "Looks like Brant's got some takers."

The other raft has pulled to river right and tucked in behind a boulder that stands fifteen feet above the water. Four of Brant's crew climb out and up the rock and jump feet first into a deep river pool. Scott explains this is to appease the river gods; get wet now and you won't have problems later.

Our boats are soon drifting together, at current speed,

through a long peaceful stretch. Helmets come off. Feet drag in the water.

I ask Scott, "Can I get out?"

"Sure."

I've been hot in the wetsuit, and the water's friendly-cool. I can feel it seeping into the suit, then warming to body temperature. It's the layer of water, not the neoprene, that insulates you.

I float on my back, holding on to the rope that runs along the side of the raft, then let go and swim away a few yards, trying to keep my feet aimed downstream and my head up high enough to see. The idea is to use your feet to kick away from the rocks as you're being swept through a rapids. Then it's a swim to the boat or the shore, if there's a beach. But, Scott has warned us, never try to stand up in whitewater. People drown fast that way. It's called entrapment; your foot gets caught under a rock and the force of the current against your back can push you facedown and under.

Lunchtime arrives. Brant helps people out of the rafts, onto the rocks: "Be careful to step above the waterline. Step only where it's dry—that's algae below and it's super-slick and you'll bust your ass quick." And Scott adds, "Poison ivy is everywhere. It's got three shiny leaves and basically everything that's green should be considered poison ivy."

The food containers are spread across a large flat rock. Roast beef and turkey slices, cheese, pasta salads, chips and salsa, peanut butter, and strawberry shortcake.

"It's ready. Ladies first." This is a practical considera-
tion, Scott tells me. If the men get in line first there's a
chance there won't be enough left for the women.

The guides wait until everyone's eating before they pick
up a plate. We stand in the sun with our sandwiches and
cups of lemonade. I meet a man from Buffalo who's trying
to sell his construction business and move to South
Carolina, but mostly the talk is about rafting and past ad-
ventures: "We hit through that first wave and I looked
back and the guide was *gone*—somehow we got the boat
on the shore down around a bend and there he comes
floating up, laughing at us."

Our laughter is edgy and comes a beat too fast. The
rapids we'll run in the next seven miles have names that are
known around the world. Some are honest Class Vs.

We load up and paddle out to midstream. Our two
boats travel close together. We pass the put-in at Cunard,
on river left. Just a few rafts are laid out there in the parking lot, getting set for an afternoon trip. From the sky
there's the thin snarl of a motor and I see Frank Thomas's
Cessna arcing across the gorge.

There's an oar-rig boat poking along the river in front of
us. It's full of Boy Scouts, who do have paddles but really
ride along as passengers. Their guide sits high in the stern
and controls the raft with two long oars. And Scott sees a
guide he knows who's out on his day off with some friends
in an old, nonbailing raft. "It's still the best," the guy says,
"still my favorite." Our raft is self-bailing. The floor is
made up of inflated tubes and it rides above the waterline,

flexing with the wave action. Any water that's inside escapes through drain holes where the floor attaches to the raft. The self-bailing raft, a fairly recent invention, saves lots of work and was instantly popular. The white plastic pickle buckets, used for bailing, stayed ashore.

Two distinct features lie ahead: we can see a railroad bridge crossing the river, and in closer focus, a distinct horizon line—a ledge that extends evenly from one bank to the other with the water disappearing over it. "A blind drop into a big hole" is how one paddler has described Upper Railroad.

We slide over the top with a whoop and for an instant we're airborne. The front of the boat kicks up high when we hit the bottom. Scott yells, "Forward! Let's see if we can do some surfing," and we zip the boat into an eddy and he turns us back upstream.

"See the hole? We'll go right on top of it."

At the edge of the river the water comes roaring off the ledge into a wide flat hydraulic. The current has so much force that it rolls back up from the rocks on the bottom and keeps on recirculating. If you were a swimmer caught in the hole you'd be in the biggest, loudest most dangerous washing machine you could imagine. Eventually, most of the time, you get kicked out and into calmer water.

We aim right at the hole—"Paddle hard"—and cross the eddy line into the blue-white churn of the hydraulic. We are facing the ledge, watching the water crash down in front of us and roll up underneath the boat to head upstream. We *surf.* Paddling just enough to keep us balanced. We're inside the spray—breathing wet white air that smells of river green.

"All back," Scott says, and we pirouette out of the hole and whirl thirty yards downriver to cruise through Middle Railroad, a smaller rapids but with some risky rocks. I watch Scott leaning far back out over the water, holding the raft on line with his paddle. Ashore, this morning at Class VI, and on the riverbank at lunchtime, Scott seemed to be of unremarkable size. But on the river when we hit the big stuff he's *huge.* And defiant—nothing's going to be a problem.

He talks with us before each rapids, telling us the name, the route we'll be taking, and what to expect if we spill out. "On this one you'll end up in a good eddy pool on the right and so will the boat." Or, "If you swim here look for a huge boulder and stay to the left of it—it's undercut."

We've passed under the bridge and now see another drop coming up: Lower Railroad. "Easy forward." We gain some momentum, moving faster than the current. We're paddling in unison and the boat moves easily.

"There's the picture guy," Scott says, "better look good."

A photographer waits, river left, on a large flat rock, two feet above the river.

Our move is on a slight angle as we approach the ledge, then over into a long, cascading plunge through a chute of boulders to the bottom. I can't hold my position on the edge of the raft and fall awkwardly into the middle again.

A Fayetteville company takes pictures of almost every raft that floats the Lower New, and the Gauley River as well. One man is at this location, most of the day. He uses a motor-drive Canon and a long lens. He has a white sun umbrella, a jug of water, and two large brown dogs curled at his feet. A film runner waits, a young man reading a paperback. Soon he'll hop in his kayak and paddle downstream and hand off the exposed rolls to a driver who'll take them into town. The pictures will be machine printed—all of them, in large format, with multiple copies—and waiting for us when we get off the bus back at Class VI. In the very early days of whitewater photography on the New, I'm told, they thought they might be able to use homing pigeons to carry the film canisters up out of the gorge to Glen Jean. But the hawks caught too many of the pigeons. In river country sometimes people will tell you things and watch your face to see how much of it you believe.

Craig asks, "Scott, is this Swimmer's Rapids up ahead? I think I want to try it."

"Go for it," Scott says. "Anybody else? Sara? Good deal."

Scott explains this is a good place to swim through a rapids without the danger of hitting rocks. Craig and Sara flip over the sides of the raft, and Carrie goes over too. Floating on their backs, they quickly move out ahead of us, navigating with their arms.

Scott yells to them, "Heads up," but the waves are high

and I can see whitewater cresting over their helmets as they jounce on down through the rapids.

We follow them, then swing into an eddy, for the pickup.

"I swallowed half the river," Craig says, coughing and laughing at the same time. Sara's gasping a bit, too. She says, "It's hard to time your breathing. You have to wait for the wave to break over you."

I regret staying in the boat. The point of decision came too fast. It would have been good experience.

· · ·

They say when you see a huge boulder in the river that looks like a whale you've arrived at The Keeneys. Or as some people call them, The Keeney Brothers. You get to noticing on this river that the mouths of creeks coincide with rapids. Here, Keeney Creek comes spilling in through a hollow from the east. And where it hits the New, the river drops. Three times. The Upper, Middle, and Lower Keeneys.

I can see Whale Rock on the left. And the river beyond that is dramatically lower than our present level. A paddler's map of the Lower Gorge says about Middle Keeney: "This is what Columbus thought would happen when he got to the edge of the world."

And my guidebook says: "Even if you are very familiar with the river, it is a good idea to get out and scout Lower Keeney. It cannot be snuck, it cannot be lined . . . so you may as well make up your mind to run it."

"Sneaking" a rapids means finding a less treacherous path; the other option involves tying a rope to the boat and walking it along the shore.

We will neither line nor sneak nor scout. Scott takes us off the current for a few minutes to talk about the Keeneys and today's high water. We'll be moving fast, he says, and the three rapids are merging; they will almost seem as one. We'll have no time to eddy out and reassess. We will aim straight forward, down the center. We check life-jacket straps and go.

The river narrows and we're pounding over two ledges and then close to Whale Rock, skidding past a strong eddy line below—at this volume of water it would be an eddy *fence* wanting to grab you and pull you under.

At Middle Keeney a bright yellow kayak cuts across our bow. The wave spray rises like sheer curtains all around ten feet high and we're yelling and the kayak rolls just in front of us and then comes back upright as we crunch over him with the front of the raft. I see the yellow flash and the kayaker's red helmet and his nose clips—the guy is grinning!

Our raft is roaring on into Lower Keeney and we're trying to add paddle power to give Scott some steering control. We drop over the first big ledge and the waves run at a diagonal from the right, pushing the boat toward Wash Up Rock. Our intention is to hold to the center, against the pressure. At the bottom of the trough the raft tilts forward, raising Scott high in the air, and I'm hit hard in the face and chest by a wave; the water almost feels solid.

Again we twirl in the bottom eddy, smiling, watching as Brant's boat comes through, almost on the same line. I now believe what we were told earlier in the day: the guide depends on the crew to get him down the river.

We float backwards down a long pool, drink some water, laugh about the screaming when we ran over the kayaker. Sara tells us she's been on whitewater out West, on the El Paso and the Rio Grande and the Gallatin, and that this is the biggest water she's seen. We're all soaked and it's turned cooler now with the sun past the rim of the gorge. I'm warm enough in the wetsuit and a fleece pullover. Scott starts passing out nylon jackets from his drybag. "Stuff left behind by clients," he says. Ellen, in shorts, is shivering, and Sara, wearing paddling pants, is kidding her. "I noticed those tanned legs," she says. "I figured you'd be sorry later." Even Scott, who says he's not bothered much by cold, pulls on a short-sleeved jacket.

We sail down Lollygag Rapids and then Dudley's Dip, both of which would have scared me earlier in the day.

Then we start hearing something bigger: Double Z is a true and consistent Class V rapids. Meaning heavy water and technical moves and *continuing* danger—it's the length of a football field.

It starts with a wall of rocks far out from the right bank. We have to make a tight turn around them and head for an eddy. Scott told us what we'd be doing but it wasn't until we were safe in the calm water that I noticed the reason: a sharp-edged undercut boulder waits in midstream. We pull out of the eddy, stay right, and drop over several ledges. At the very bottom is Pour Over Rock, which, again, I don't appreciate until I see it from downstream. The upper side is level with the waves so you could easily run out on the flat surface and then tumble over a cliff.

A few more rapids to run, then a long, slow turn and the New River Bridge comes into view. It is a mile downstream when we first see it, and a thousand feet above the water. As we get closer the bridge appears to drift across the sky, at a cloud's pace.

The old Fayette Station bridge, which still stands, was built at regular river level, set across stone pilings. And you can see the relevant topography, and the problem. The highway loops down one very steep side of the gorge, crosses the New, then starts up the opposite—very steep—side of the gorge. From cliff edge to cliff edge it was a forty-minute drive. Now it's forty seconds.

Scott tells us, "A couple of years ago they bungeed off a GMC Jimmy from that bridge. You might have seen the commercial."

We ask, "They pushed a GMC Jimmy off the bridge on bungee cords?"

"Yep. It looked great on TV. But they left the thing hanging there for a long time after the shoot. We kind of got used to coming around this corner of the river and seeing it up there. They tell me they had offered the truck to the guy who rigged the shot, local guy; he set up the bungee cords and made sure everything would hold. They wanted him to ride in it down off the bridge as they filmed and if he'd do it they'd give him the Jimmy."

Our boat moves fifty yards on the water before we ask, "Well?"

"He said no. They pushed it over empty."

. . .

Fayette Station Rapids waits just below the original bridge. It's our last run of the day and we move through it nicely, bouncing in some big holes. It's deceptive—doesn't look scary. But a champion high school swimmer dropped off the bridge one day, without a life vest, and drowned. The wave action is so strong you just can't fight your way back up from the bottom.

Jon Dragan, who started the first rafting company, Wildwater Expeditions Unlimited, told me he was afraid to run Fayette Station, back in the sixties. "We'd pull in by the bridge and call it a trip; sleep till morning and drive home to Pennsylvania. All the locals said you'd die in there. Then one night we were drinking around the fire and promised ourselves we'd try it in the morning and so we did. Thirty years later we're still doing it."

Back at Class VI in late afternoon it's a good feeling to take a long, steamy hot shower and put on dry clothes and stand out on the terrace as the other trip groups come back in. Reminds me of the late Friday nights after high school football games, when you'd walk out of the locker room with wet hair, tired, happy.

For supper I decide to have a white pizza and a salad at Bazil's in Fayetteville. And I see a familiar face as I walk in. I'd met Dave Arnold after we got back today; he's one of the owners of Class VI. He's here for pizza with his wife, Peggy, and their three-year-old son, Jeffrey.

Dave said, "Sit and join us. I was wondering what you were going to do for dinner, but you've made the right choice."

Peggy had been teaching middle and high school and is now home for Jeffrey's first years. Dave's work these days is in the office, mostly on the phone, but he gets on the water as much as he can. He started in the business as a raft guide and still leads trips on the New and the Gauley.

I show him my river photograph. The pictures from Lower Railroad were on sale at Class VI. It was $16.95 for a large color print, and there were five shots to choose from.

Dave says, "This company's really got it dialed in. The key to it is—the picture's right there for you to take home. You don't fool around with looking at slides or a contact sheet and filling out an order form. In the wintertime they're taking ski pictures, all over the country, just the same way."

I explain, "I might have chosen the wrong picture here. I'll see how it looks when I get home."

I'd picked a shot that shows me hesitating. I'm leaning to the inside of the raft, and of the seven of us in the boat I'm the only one with his paddle out of the water.

"I thought this might be a good reminder."

Dave laughs. "Could be a lot worse. I've seen pictures of guys climbing naked back in the boat—they lose their shorts in the rapids."

And he asks how my trip went, saying, "I notice you're still smiling. I see that a lot. Who was your guide today? Were you on Scott's boat?"

I tell him how impressed I was with Scott, and how I'd get right back in the same boat at first light tomorrow if I had a chance.

"Did Scott mention the trial? I just wondered."

"No."

Dave says, "We just finished a trial here at the courthouse. We had a fatality on the river in 1992, and we were sued for wrongful death. It was Scott's boat and he had to testify. It was a unanimous verdict: not guilty. But I know he's been torn up about it."

"What happened?"

"Four people flipped out in Middle Keeney. One of them swam through Lower Keeney and was picked up. Two managed to stay above the rapids and they were okay. Joy Marr was the trip leader that day; she had to testify, too. A woman from Scott's boat got caught in between some rocks, in a strainer, we call it, where the water's pouring through a crack—it's an incredible force and she was face into it under the surface. They got her out, took her to Beckley by helicopter, did all they could including heart massage, nothing worked."

Dave continued, "The trial when it finally came was

reassuring. It showed just how careful we are and how well the people are trained. Scott risked his life in that water, walking across rafts to get a line on her life jacket. We've taken 350,000 people down the river since we started and had, now, two deaths. The other one was a heart attack, a guy on the bus coming back, but that could have happened anywhere."

We talk a little more, about mountain biking and music, and other rivers and towns, then say good-bye on the sidewalk outside Bazil's.

I walk for an hour on the quiet streets of Fayetteville, letting the last of the adrenaline ease away. I have a bruised, banged-up hand, and my left leg is strained and aching; it was my anchor leg in the raft.

29

CANYON RIM

38° 05′N
81° 05′W

You can hear the music from out in the road well enough to know that it's stuff from a couple of decades ago. There's a bass throb through the trees and you remember nights like this when you might have gotten in trouble. I park the Jeep and start walking faster when the band starts playing "The Weight": "I pulled into Nazareth, was feeling about half-past dead. . . ."

This is the end-of-season staff party at Class VI. A cool Sunday night with an early October three-quarter moon. You'd be comfortable in shorts and sandals, but with socks and a pullover. The river people are tanned, tired, smiling.

The musicians are set up on the low wooden porch of the wetsuit room; it's a black neoprene and pink and blue nylon backdrop. The lead singer is standing behind a double set of keyboards. There's a bass player and a drummer, helped out by a happy raft guide sitting on the steps playing a couple of overturned plastic buckets.

Some of the leftover Gauley customers wander out of the shower room, pick up a beer from the icy washtub and a barbeque sandwich, and probably think, *Damn, this place is all right!*

All the buses are in, all today's boaters are back safe. A few more river trips remain on the schedule, there's a month's work yet to do getting the equipment ready for the spring, but tonight feels like the real end. The muscles around the back of the neck loosen, the month-long low-grade headache starts to fade. A UHF radio is switched off, left in a bag.

The band plays "Mustang Sally," and several couples dance out on the flagstone walk. Some of the guides do the West Virginia cool hustle; you just stand in front of the band with a can of beer and a cigarette and sort of jive around.

Stories float above the music. . . . A guide came back one morning at dawn wet and trembling with cold. He and his friends had been trying a moonlight river run and it got overcast and they didn't have sleeping bags or even flashlights and had to sleep out on the rocks, tucked into the dew-covered rafts. . . . A mom had taken the kids down to the Gauley to watch the boats come through Pillow Rock Rapids and along the way they saw fresh piles of sweet-smelling bear gorge. The bears eat the apples in the old orchards, eat too fast and too many, and throw up. . . . A young videoboater, who will soon be at Harvard Divinity School, describes a close call that afternoon, sweeping his hands through the air.

The band kicks off "Rikki Don't Lose That Number," and the people laughing are the ones who heard it when it was new. The Class VI staff now has twenty years together, and many of them have been around since the start. They grin and hug each other and dance close for a night, barefoot and wearing tight jeans. There are mothers and dads holding babies, and three-year-olds running around.

Jeff Proctor, one of the owners, says, "I love these parties. We're like a farming community and it's harvest time. Everyone else has left and these are the people that made it possible."

And he says, "Ten years ago this would've gone on until two o'clock in the morning."

The singer starts an old Gram Parsons song about the truckers and the kickers and the cowboy angels; it even mentions a river bridge—and if there's to be a happy-sad moment of the evening, it arrives now:

> *Won't you scratch my itch, sweet Annie Rich*
> *And welcome me back to town . . .*
>
> *And I saw my devil,*
> *And I saw my deep blue sea*
> *And I thought about a calico bonnet from*
> *Cheyenne to Tennessee . . .*
> *Oh, but I remembered something you once told me*
> *And I'll be damned if it did not come true*
> *Twenty thousand roads I went down, down down*
> *And they all lead me straight back to you.*

30

NEW RIVER BRIDGE

38° 04′N
81° 05′W

You would think of San Francisco, to see this bridge on a morning when there's fog in the Lower Gorge, *except* that here all the structure is below the roadway, not above. It's a single span, arching from one cliff to the other. The steel is designed to rust, so it won't need painting; the bridge has an autumnal color. The fog can be a satiny white, layered just under the roadway, and flowing downriver at a speed, which, I suspect, would match that of the water, far below.

This is Bridge Day. It's a festival that happens every October, on the third Saturday. They barricade the two northbound lanes, and the police watch over two-way traffic on the southbound side.

So I am *walking* out over the New River Gorge, starting to feel a faint trembling through the concrete and steel, even though the trucks and cars are moving at a respectful speed on the other side of the barrier.

Gene and Maura Kistler have a house fairly close; when the wind's right they can hear the high-speed whine from the bridge. Gene's a rock climber; Maura's a kayaker. Back in more adventurous times they would climb out under the bridge in the dark night, creep along a walkway, and tuck themselves up into one of the expansion joints—narrow open steel gratings between sections of concrete. They would lie on their backs and look up at the stars . . . and hear an eighteen-wheeler keening down the grade and out onto the three-thousand-foot-long bridge. They could hear the other gratings as the truck approached. A faraway *whoomph*. Then closer: *whoomph*. And in quick seconds: *WHOOMPH!* Then the truck would *crush* by, directly above their faces. The Kistlers don't go out under the bridge at night anymore; they've started a family.

Bridge Day is an extreme-sports festival. There's a street fair—food and music and crafts and T-shirts—that provides a neighborly stage for a drama that is played out at center bridge. A flatbed truck trailer has been pulled tight alongside the railing. Three plywood ramps have been built, tilting up from the trailer and out over the rail. Parachute jumpers, hundreds of them, will be leaping off those ramps and into the airspace of the New River Gorge. The altitude of the bridge is 1,586 feet. The altitude of the sandbar where the jumpers try to land is 710 feet. If the parachute were not to open, the fall would be eight seconds long.

The view into the gorge begins to clear as the sun warms the fog. I've come early, and brought coffee along, and binoculars, for a wait at the railing, facing upriver. Within an hour the first boats appear; five of them, cruising around a bend. White rafts, red helmets—it's the Class VI dawn trip. The company takes pride in being first down the river on Bridge Day, and this group started paddling in the dark. They'll make it through Fayette Station Rapids, staying to the right, then cross to the flat sandy bank for lunch and parachute viewing.

The jumping is soon to begin, but it seems I'm downwind of the cooking and it might be wise to make an early pass along the rows of tables and tents and trailers. If your child would like his face painted in camouflage, that's possible. There's also FREE FACE PAINTING WITH BIBLE STORIES. T-shirts that say IF YOU'RE NOT LIVIN' ON THE EDGE, YOU'RE TAKIN' UP TOO MUCH SPACE. Or a BASE shirt that shows three jumpers, arms and legs outstretched, in the sky just below the bridge. Plus the equation: $Y=V_0 T+1/2\ AyT^2$ and the impact speed, 163 m.p.h. Another T-shirt: SKY DIVERS—GOOD TO THE LAST DROP.

There is a booth with sweet-potato french fries drizzled with butter and brown sugar, but I keep walking until I see my canoeing friend Joy Marr in an apron. Back on the Upper New she told me about the grilled marinated turkey-breast fajitas that she and her friend Cindy Abbot make for Bridge Day. Here they are, flushed by the heat from the grill and already almost sold out. I walk away with a half-pound lunch.

Five men who look to be still tough but well retired are sitting in lawn chairs under an awning, and a sign: WELCOME BRIDGE WORKERS. One of them is talking with a young boy, and his dad, who's videotaping the conversation. It's a reunion of some of the workers who helped put this bridge together twenty years ago. One man was killed during that construction, when a platform fell. In the years since, three people have been killed, in various sport jumps, on Bridge Day.

As I walk back toward the center of the bridge I see the first parachutists going off the ramps over the railing. They do jump outwards, for clearance, but then they fall straight down and it's a deadweight drop. It's sudden and eerie; it has the look of a body dropping from the gallows. From this angle you can't see the parachutes pop and blossom.

BASE means building, antenna, span, earth. You try to achieve all four and then keep on doing all of it all over again. BASE jumpers in Norway, or Germany, or Japan, know they can come to West Virginia in October and have legal access to a world-class-height bridge and safety support below.

I move up to the flatbed trailer to watch the jumpers going off the ramps. They're waiting in a fast-moving line. They step up on the trailer and get their equipment checked by the jumpmaster: he jerks hard against the buckles, makes sure they have a pilot chute. And then the jumpers, on the balls of their feet at the very edge, wait to scream and disappear.

They all have competent-looking apparatus: the main parachute with shoulder and leg web harnesses, and the smaller pilot chute, which is gathered high in one hand, and, when released, will pull out the larger one. Some jumpers have video recorders mounted on their helmets, with the red light glowing. Some are wearing cameras and holding a shutter-release cable.

And they are all interesting-looking people. The ones who are in ordinary clothes—jacket, lime Lycra tights, orange climbing boots—have flashing eyes and fleeting smiles. But some are masked and wearing full costumes: Spiders from Mars, and a Pumpkin Man, and a Jester in fuchsia and orange. There's also a guy with a week's growth of dark beard, a *lit* cigar, and a Santa Claus hat.

From my perspective at the railing, about a hundred yards away from the trailer, I can see the jumpers leap away from the bridge and fall chest first: two seconds, three, then four, then the chute's out—a bright, striped parasail chute—and the landing glide begins. Sometimes it's a contented swirl and drift. Sometimes it's a tense, fast swoop, with too-late corrections.

The target is a circle of stones on the riverbank, to the right from the jumper's view. There are swift-water rescue teams waiting, in rafts with motors affixed. The idea is to flare down and feather out across the river, rising then slightly to the bank. Your feet touch first—a few steps and you're in the circle with your chute spilling behind. Some jumpers skip on the water before making the bank. Others dump directly into the river, with the rescue raft already approaching. A few others spin off into the spindly birch trees. There are EMS units waiting as well.

One jumper on the bridge, while repacking his chute for leap number three, tells a story from last year. It seems the wind was up that day and a guy lost control and went way off course into the trees. He ended up with a branch in his rectum; they had to cut him out of the tree to take him to the hospital, "And he's back this year. I just saw him; he's going to try it again."

That evening in Fayetteville I asked several people about the jumper in the trees and the chainsaw and the hospital and everyone said, "Oh yeah, I heard about that last year. That's true."

31

HAWKS NEST

38° 07′N
81° 06′w

A river friend has told me, "You gotta get down in the Drys. There's just no way to understand that river unless you see that. That's where the biggest rapids *ever* would be—but the water's all shut off."

I stood on the cliff's edge at Hawks Nest State Park, looking back upriver; the high bridge would be in sight were it not for a bend or two. Just below that bridge, there's a final, friendly rapids called Flea Flicker—it's the last whitewater on the New River unless a hurricane passes through.

From Flea Flicker down to the Hawks Nest Dam, the river is a gently moving, curving lake, filling the deep channel between the mountains. CSX railroad tracks run along both sides, with a few fishing cabins on the strips of land between the rails and the river. There's no road; you're supposed to get in by boat but they say most people walk the tracks.

The water itself, in the reservoir behind the dam, and especially from this height, shows clear and greenish blue, with bounces of yellows and reds from the changing leaves. The fall *turnover*—a biologist's term—has occurred; back in midsummer's heat the river here is brown. In a lake or a reservoir the top layer of water, warmed by the sun, lies atop a cooler layer. The demarcation between them is called a thermocline. In the fall as the top water cools the two layers reach toward equal temperature. One day, that happens and the thermocline disappears. The balance is held, for a moment, for an hour, until a good fresh breeze stirs the surface and the water swirls and flips and the nutrients from the bottom find the top and kick off a phytoplankton bloom. That day has come on the New—hearty green organisms having a feast.

Below the cliff the river comes almost to a full stop against the Hawks Nest Dam, a concrete structure that spans the bottom two-thirds of the gorge. Gauley Mountain rises on river right, a massive landmark of crests and creases. There is a tunnel that's been cut through the mountain; it diverts the river for a fast fall to the turbines of a power station. The electricity goes to a metallurgical plant.

If you study the history of America's industrial tragedies, you'll find perhaps not enough mention of the Hawks Nest Tunnel.

Construction began in 1930, during desperate times. Hubert Skidmore wrote a novel about the project and its

aftermath. He opens his book, *Hawk's Nest,* with this pro-
logue:

> As autumn gave way to winter, the nights chilling
> the hills beneath their bright covers, more and
> more men found their way into West Virginia. Out
> of the South and out of the East they came, and
> out of Joplin, Missouri, and Picher, Oklahoma,
> searching their way toward the rocky, irregular state.
> Depression-ridden and work-hungry, they set out,
> leaving their families behind with the great chat
> piles; crushed rock from which the ore had been re-
> moved. And no coal. They sat in the kitchen by the
> gas stove and the wife cried, watching the flame,
> afraid it would stop. They only bought what they
> couldn't live without, knowing the A & P man on
> Lake Street extended their credit out of his own
> pocket. "Ralph went to West Virginia, looking for
> work. We want to pay every cent we owe."
>
> "I'll send for you and the young-uns. First regular
> pay, I'll send for you and the young-uns."

· · ·

These days there's not much to see down by the dam, and
heavy wire fences keep you from getting close. From upstream you can spot the intake gate where the tunnel starts
into Gauley Mountain. Tall rusting steel doors can be low-
ered to control the flow.

On the map, the Gauley Bridge quadrangle, you notice the tunnel because it's a broad straight white line with blue dashes, bypassing a horseshoe bend in the New, then aligning once more with the river, before cutting off two more bends on its final run to the power plant. The tunnel is three miles long. On the map it is labeled an "aqueduct." Old photographs show the inside as a craggy, round cavern, diminishing to blackness. It was cut by pick and shovel, by drill and dynamite blast. And because the mountain is almost pure silica, it was a deadly place to work.

I talked with a tunnel survivor, close to twenty years ago, on his front porch in the town of Gauley Bridge, downriver. When he hired on to the Hawks Nest project he was a young man, and lucky. Many of his co-worker friends died within a few years, some died while they were still on the job. He told me about coming in from a day in the tunnel, his clothes white with silica dust, and about coughing and streams of thick mucus coming from his nose: "It was like white toothpaste."

The danger of silicosis was known at the time. Potters in Britain had damaged lungs, and gold miners in South Africa. It had been seen among the zinc miners in Missouri. The silicosis threat inside Gauley Mountain was far more acute. It struck the tunnel workers like a silent, shadowy thunderbolt.

The men were cutting through sandstone that had a silica content over 90 percent. That fact delighted Union

Carbide, the company that was building the tunnel. It meant that in addition to the promise of abundant electrical power, Union Carbide now owned a silica mine. From the *Fayetteville Tribune,* June 1931:

> Like a tale from the story of Aladdin's lamp, boring of the tunnel has enriched the Union Carbide company with untold wealth. In the process of removing the rock, the workers came upon a deposit of silica sandstone which assays 99.44 percent pure. It is as fine a grade of sandstone and especially adaptable for steel and glass work, as has been found in the world.

I decide to go for a walk in the Drys. I put on a jacket against a good breeze, and take along a walking stick. And I'm wearing my river sandals with the sticky bottoms, mostly because I talked with a raft guide this morning who got through the whole season fine but wrenched his ankle making a wrong step coming down out of his camper.

It's an easy fishing trail down from a gravel road, and a clamber over the rocks and out onto the flat slabs of the riverbed. It looks like Arizona; the rocks are bleached tans and grays, with indentations holding clear green sheets of water. A trickle of the New is spilling down from the dam but it quickly loses continuity. A kayak might work here, but only for twenty or thirty yards at a time before you'd be carrying it.

There's a sign on the bank: WARNING. ĐAM UPSTREAM.

WATER MAY RISE RAPIDLY AT ANY TIME. WITHOUT WARN-
ING. SIREN WILL WARN OF DEFINITE WATER RISE. AVOID
PLACING YOURSELF WHERE QUICK EXIT FROM RIVER IS
DIFFICULT.

I walk on downriver, balancing from rock to rock, sometimes along a gravelly beach. A couple of times the boulders are so large I have to wade around them, in water up to my waist. And once I slip and crack an elbow hard on the way down. I'm at a point where the canyon walls are steep and the road above is out of shouting range.

The New River can rampage through here. It happens once or twice every few years when the rains come heavy upstream. They let excess water out of Bluestone Dam, fifty miles away. They open the gates of the Hawks Nest Dam, and then this dusty section of the New becomes scary, supreme whitewater. It's the steepest drop on the river, through the Drys, and I can see house-sized boulders and jagged shelves of shale, angled upstream.

It was a fellow named Michael Ivey who first told me about the Drys. He grew up nearby and became a river guide—everyone called him "Spike." Back when he was learning and the water was up in the Drys, Michael used to put on his paddling gear and come out here to hitch a ride on any raft going. He'd say, "Hey, my buddies haven't shown up. Can I ride with you?"

And a few years later on a day when all of West Virginia was in flood and cows were getting swept away and caught up in the bridges, Michael and two friends put a raft in the river at the top of the Drys. The New River is fast at five feet, dangerous at seven, eight, or nine feet. This day it was twenty-eight feet.

Michael said, "We were deep in the gorge and it was big, hungry water. There were fifty-five-gallon drums floating in there. Scott was already hurting; we had him in the center to bail. Roger and I had paddles. There's only two rapids in the Drys. The first one's a mile long. Seems ten miles long. Right away we tried to slide between two holes and I got kicked out. You really take a bashing. I was going down on the eddy wall; the life jacket busted and my arm came out. I was freaking out real deep in a nasty, gritty, black river."

I asked Michael, "Are you consciously aware that you can't take a breath? That you have to get back up before you breathe?"

"Oh, yeah, that's experience. But you doubt you'll make it and you get confused and panicky about where you are. I got recirculated back up and it was almost too late. People talk about 'seeing God' in that situation. I was going to the light. Luckily it was sunlight shining down through the muddy water."

"I still can't understand why you'd try it, the river that high?"

"Well, you know you've got the skills and you know the rush is there. It's like playing a super video game, only the stakes are much higher. How does it get any better than that? I went home that night and my wife was watching television—they happened to be showing *Deliverance,* and those guys are going down that river in Georgia and we're watching and across the bottom of the screen comes this warning about severe flood conditions in the following counties and telling people to move to higher ground and the most rewarding thing is that I'm the guy who was *there.* We were riding that flood."

. . .

Another large sign: FIVE MINUTES AFTER THE SIREN BE-GINS TO SOUND HIGH WATER WILL BE RELEASED.

A lot of people must come this way fishing. The riverbed here is like a cliff laid down sideways. There are spiderwebs across some crevices, rainwater trapped in others. A dry red maple leaf will swing down through the air, or one of the big tulip poplar leaves, now yellow. There's a cave cutting back under one of the boulders and it's filled with a tangle of dead trees and rusted strands of fencing wire.

Local legend has it that when men would die on the Hawks Nest Tunnel job, they'd be taken out and thrown in the river, with rocks tied to their bodies. A man might have a family, in a tarpaper shack in one of the camps. No one would tell his wife, he just wouldn't come home. The next morning she'd be told to leave.

The company denied there was a problem with silica dust, even though Carbide officials who toured the job site would have to wear respirators. The company blamed poor nutrition and said the men would stand around in bad weather in front of open fires, gambling, and that Negroes were especially prone to catch pneumonia.

Pneumonia was indeed a cause of death. The tiny silica particles are absorbed by cells in the lung. The lungs are scarred. Breathing becomes more difficult, disease comes easily.

Martin Cherniak, a physician and occupational medicine specialist, wrote a book about the project, *The Hawk's Nest Incident.* He sums up his research with this estimate of death: "Within five years after its completion, the Hawk's Nest Tunnel would have claimed a total of 764 victims to silicosis, or to other less provocatively named causes of death from dusty lungs."

The legal struggles for settlement stretched on for decades. But soon you won't be able to find people, the old people in Gauley Bridge, who can tell you about the ambulances and their silent daily trips up over the mountain.

32

GAULEY BRIDGE

38° 09'N
81° 11'W

I've spent some time walking among tombstones in the cemetery at Gauley Bridge. It's on a hillside above the town. From there you can see the main highway, next to the railroad tracks, and then the New River, with the Gauley flowing in from the east out of its own narrow-cut valley.

It's an old cemetery and many of the stones are weather-worn and tilted. Some are tiny, for infants, and one of those has a carved lamb lying across the top.

Matilda Baldwin was buried here in 1854. Thomas Cavendish in 1885. Carrie, born May 10, 1840, the wife of William Tyree. Frank Messer, who died in 1888. Woodrow Messer: he served in WW II with the 44th Armored Cavalry. And the names drift on across the grass: Huddleston, Hughart, Winebrenner, Keiffer, Adcock, Whetsell. . . . People have left flowers on some of the graves, and only a few are plastic. Often these days you'll see the everbright yellows and red and whites—gumdrop cemeteries, I call them.

Back up in the gorge, there are many abandoned, almost forgotten burial sites. A friend took me to see one of them, close by the river; he asked me not to write about its precise location. Coming upon it you have a sense of cared-for landscape. The trees are small—birches and pines—and well spaced. The ground is covered by myrtle—periwinkle, it's called; it was often planted in cemeteries. You begin to see outlines of sunken graves. A few river rocks serve for tombstones, and some metal markers, the kind supplied by the funeral homes. Also a leather work boot, nailed to a post. This is a coal miners' cemetery; many of the graves belong to men who died in an explosion.

And there are lovely family graveyards out in the country, often enclosed by stone walls. If you're lucky you'll sit on the porch of the original homestead and hear an old man tell stories: "My grandfather was Captain Joel Houghton Abbot. He fought with the 8th Virginia Cavalry for four years and, man, that was a rough four years. They didn't have any place to sleep and they didn't carry any bedrolls, just a little saddlebag and I imagine they had a half-gallon of whiskey in that. Now *his* father was the one who first came here. He had a basket business—hickory baskets. I have his diary. He went all over the East selling baskets. If he had a twenty-dollar bill that was big money and, hell, he was gone to New York or to Europe."

. . .

Seven years ago I went back to my own father's family home, in Kentucky, three counties west of the New River Valley. I drove along a ridge looking for the smallest dot on the map. A man sitting on a road grader said, "There used to be an Adams post office in a store up there but now that's gone too."

"Is there a cemetery?" I asked.

"Sure, just over the hill."

The graveyard at Adams was next to the road. There were about fifty headstones. I wrote down some names: Tackett, Wilson, Bledsoe, Ball . . . and I had forgotten my father was buried here.

We hadn't been close when he died. I'd gone to the funeral more out of duty than love, arrived late, and barely remember the church and procession to the cemetery. I've kept no image of the gravesite, and when I saw the bronze tablet set in gray marble I thought I might fall. I had been hiding from this moment for twenty years.

> Roy G. Adams
> Kentucky FCS 2 US Navy World War II Korea
> November 1, 1914–July 9, 1973

. . .

This is my last day on the New River, an afternoon's wandering by canoe. There's a camping park on the riverbank, mostly trailers—a couple of construction guys might live here Monday evening through Friday morning before driving home on the weekend. I stopped at the office and paid two dollars to put in at a sandy beach, in shallow clear water.

It's good to be paddling my own boat once again. I'll be going up the river so it could be tricky; it's wide here and the current appears slow but there's a strong push coming down.

My first stop is out in midstream. I've wanted to get a closer look at two very large rocks, each standing thirty feet high in the center of the New, just before its junction with the Gauley. Three crosses rise above one of the rocks. They are made from notched and fitted timbers. Two are painted pale blue and the one standing tallest in the center is Jerusalem gold. The colors were chosen by Bernard Coffindaffer of Craigsville, West Virginia. He accumulated $2 million from mining and by collecting waste oil from gas stations: "God gave it to me to make money."

His cross-erecting mission began in 1982 after his heart surgery. He sends out two-man crews and they've put up more than a thousand cross clusters on donated land, usually along highways, mostly in West Virginia, Maryland, Virginia.

When Bernard Coffindaffer passed through Gauley Bridge one day he looked out at the river and stopped his car and told a policeman, "I'm seizing that rock for Jesus of Nazareth. Don't let anything happen to it. I'll be back." Two days later his men started drilling into the rock. The job took a week.

The neighboring rock, upstream, was already spoken for. Situated on top is an old blue bus. It has a front porch overlooking a rocky yard and wooden steps leading down to a dock. There's a TV antenna, and power and phone lines reaching across to the Gauley Bridge side of the river.

This is Bruiser Cole's place. It's said they made him put the porch on the front so it would look more like a fishing camp than a school bus. It's said that five West Virginia governors in a row have personally asked Mr. Cole to remove his bus, the state's opinion being that it's a disgrace. And when tourists stop in town they hear the story that the bus got out on the rock because one day in spring flood it washed off a road and down the Gauley and out into the New and marooned itself there. Truth is, Mr. Cole bought the worn-out school bus and carried it to the rock on a barge and made it his hideaway in full view of the town of Gauley Bridge. He has a regular home, I'm told, up on Scrabble Creek. "He's a little mean," people would say. "He may not want to talk to you."

I intend to visit and see if he'd invite me to sit on the porch and talk some about the river, but I don't dare get any closer than ten feet away from his dock. I paddle around a bit, yelling up at the bus, "Hello. Mr. Cole? Hello?"

If there'd been a skiff tied off to a pole at his landing I might've stayed but it looks like Bruiser Cole is somewhere between his island and Scrabble Creek, so I push on upriver.

I have to pull deep and hard with each stroke. The wind is on my back; I can feel it on my left ear. I'm not sure I could take my canoe very far upstream against a facing wind.

I'm trying to reach the power plant, where the Hawks Nest Tunnel comes in and the New is allowed to return to its natural bed. The current shoves the bow offline to my right and I correct with the paddle, but it's tough to stay in midstream so I head to the edge of the river and then follow the ducks, paddling upstream from one tree-snag eddy pool to the next.

There's a false sense of motion, moving against the current. It's like being inside an airplane, still parked at the gate, and seeing another plane slide past outside the window; part of the world is moving but you're not.

I cross under a blackened railroad trestle perched on sandstone pedestals. The structure seems improbably narrow. You'd sure know when a train was getting close; the valley sounds, sliding across the water, have an amplified clarity. And I can feel the tremors from the coal trucks coming off Gauley Mountain, straining down through the gears.

The power plant has a sign: BOATERS KEEP OUT DANGER TURBULENT WATER. The building is of elegant masonry, with turbine machinery visible through tall clerestory windows. A mother and her son, fishing, are out on a narrow walkway between the windows and above the easy rush from the tunnel. There are flashes of white as the diverted water meets the river.

I have lunch on the riverbank. The ledges are scribed with pale green lichens. Virginia creeper vines climb the small willows, flame red against gold. A heart is carved into a tree, an endearment to TONYA: 5–14–94. And painted on a boulder: THE BRIDGE—'77. If you were growing up in Gauley Bridge this would be a late-night beer-drinking and campfire place.

The Italian carvings are close by. Walk up from the water, keep looking down, and you'll find ITALIAN, in block letters, cut with a chisel and mallet into a flat expanse of stone. There's also a Christian cross. And the carving known locally as The Mariner, a drawing of a seaman standing behind a ship's wheel. Someone has added paint to make the image bolder; the mariner's eyes and hat are blue and the wheel is blue with red spokes. Stonemasons from Italy made these carvings in the late 1800s. They'd come to West Virginia for work on the railroads.

· · ·

The light on the river is now from the west. The October sun will pass beyond the ridge in late afternoon, hours before full dark. I take the boat to the middle of the New, to a place where it is almost still. Ahead, I can see the faster waters of the Gauley, entering from the right.

At this confluence the New and the Gauley are ended. They become the Kanawha River, which gives way to the Ohio. I could paddle on downstream past the chemical plants and steel mills of the Kanawha Valley, turn left at

Point Pleasant and follow the Ohio to Huntington and Catlettsburg, take out on river left at Ashland, and walk five blocks up the hill to the white frame house where I grew up.

.   .   .

I hold the canoe in the last slight ripples of the New River. My trip down from Snake Mountain is over. The maps make sense to me; I understand the green, brown, and blue lines of terrain and watercourse. But I am in deeper wonder now about the settlers. Could *I* have come from England, from Ireland, Germany, Poland, for land, or out of desperation? What *would* the Civil War have meant? Wouldn't I have been thrilled, too, by the railroads and the coal? How strong could I have been when the Depression tore through the valleys? We are left with the mysteries of our own people. The answers lie in these graves, and deep in these waters, long passed.

UPDATE

Most of my traveling on and along the New took place in the spring, summer, and fall of 1997. I've returned to many places, many times since, to visit friends and see the river again.

Ed Greene, the Appalachian State biologist, has passed away. Lowell Shipe has moved the Whitetop Laurel Fly Shop into the town of West Jefferson. Shawn Hash and his wife, Molly, closed their Java River coffeeshop in Radford but continue to operate Tangent Outfitters. Shawn is recovering from a severe leg fracture—an avalanche accident in Colorado. Joy Marr competed in the *Raid Gauloises* in Ecuador—a four-hundred-mile multi-sport endurance race—as a member of the only American team to finish. She's involved in adventure-race training and still operates a catering business. Truman Dent has left his campground business at Thayer, and his memorabilia collection is dispersed. (I did, finally, get a chance to sit by the river and talk with him about his coal-mining days.)

In 1998, the New was designated as one of fourteen American Heritage Rivers; President Clinton traveled to Ashe County for the ceremony.

The New River Trail State Park is no longer closed between miles 17 and 19. A court-assisted settlement was reached in 1999 and now it's fifty-seven straight-through miles for biking or hiking.

My companions on the Lower Gorge whitewater raft trip weren't aware that I might write about this adventure, so I changed their names in the text. I haven't seen them back on the river, but I'd be pleased to paddle with them any time.

Fayetteville's ten-cent parking meters have been removed. The parking's free, but you're only supposed to stay in one spot for an hour. The Cathedral Cafe now has a new owner, but, thankfully, Kim's secret whole-grain pancake recipe was part of the deal.

N.D.A.
October 2000

ACKNOWLEDGMENTS

Along with those mentioned in the text, my thanks go to river friends Pat Beaver and Robert Creed of Appalachian State University, Katy Miller of the National Park Service, and Paul and Michelle Shaw in Fayetteville.

For editorial help: Tom Spain, Beth Rashbaum, and Andrea Nicolay. Neenah Ellis provided cartographical analysis, along with Harry Zohn of the U.S. Geological Survey. For continuing years of encouragement, my agent Jonathon Lazear.

National Public Radio allowed me to disappear for many months, and once again I thank Ellen Weiss of *All Things Considered*.

REFERENCES AND READING

Over the years I've gathered a few hundred "mountain books," as the librarians at Berea College like to call them. All these volumes have been useful, in the way that rainfall becomes creekflow and river current. For this work I've drawn specifically from an important few.

My title comes from *Our Southern Highlanders,* by Horace Kephart (University of Tennessee Press). This is an early account of pioneer life in and around the Great Smoky Mountains, the land that Kephart called "Back of Beyond," or "Far Appalachia."

For other history: *Miners, Millhands, and Mountaineers: Industrialization of the Appalachian South, 1880–1930,* by Ronald D Eller (University of Tennessee Press); *Trans-Allegheny Pioneers: Historical Sketches of the First White Settlements West of the Alleghenies,* by John P. Hale (Roberta Ingles Steele, Radford, Virginia); *Albion's Seed: Four British Folkways in America,* by David Hackett Fischer (Oxford University Press); *A Shorter Illustrated History of Ulster,* by Jonathan Bardon (The Blackstaff Press, Belfast); *Trail of Tears: The Rise and Fall of the Cherokee Nation,* by John Ehle (Anchor Books); *Daniel Boone: The Life and Legend of an American Pioneer,* by John Mack Faragher (Henry Holt); *The*

Melungeons: The Resurrection of a Proud People, by N. Brent Kennedy (Mercer University Press).

For natural history: *The Dying of the Trees: The Pandemic in America's Forests,* by Charles E. Little (Viking); *Travels of William Bartram,* edited by Mark Van Doren (Dover); *Another Country: Journeying Toward the Cherokee Mountains,* by Christopher Camuto (Henry Holt); *Hollows, Peepers, and Highlanders: An Appalachian Mountain Ecology,* by George Constantz (Mountain Press, Missoula, Montana); *Wildflowers of the Southern Appalachians,* by Kevin Adams and Marty Casstevens (John F. Blair, Winston-Salem, North Carolina).

An invaluable guide has been *New River: A Photographic Essay,* by Arnout Hyde, Jr. (Cannon Graphics, Inc., Charleston, West Virginia). Also *Classic Virginia Rivers,* by Ed Grove (Eddy Out Press, Arlington, Virginia), and *Wildwater West Virginia,* by Paul Davidson, Ward Eister, Dirk Davidson, Charlie Walbridge (Menasha Ridge Press, Birmingham, Alabama).

Two documentaries have been useful: the story of Ivanhoe, Virginia, as told in *Rough Side of the Mountain,* directed by Anne Lewis (Appalshop, Whitesburg, Kentucky), and *Point Man for God,* produced by Jacob Young (WNPB-TV, Morgantown, West Virginia), which is about Bernard Coffindaffer and his crosses.

I've found two historical novels to be especially compelling: *The Winter People,* by John Ehle (Harper & Row) and *Storming Heaven,* by Denise Giardina (Ivy Books).

ABOUT THE AUTHOR

NOAH ADAMS is a co-host of NPR's *All Things Considered.* He lives with his wife, Neenah Ellis, a freelance journalist, in Takoma Park, Maryland.

Printed in the United States
by Baker & Taylor Publisher Services